'If we can leave sentiment aside, you're well out of this club, Darren. They'll always be selling to survive, not buying to succeed.'

Darren couldn't deny the point. His mind was in turmoil. He felt like he'd been picked up by a whirlwind and didn't know where on earth he'd be dumped by it. Then another thought occurred.

'What about the damage a move would do to any England career I might have?'

'If you succeed over there it will *enhance* your international prospects!' Nick answered slickly.

'But I'm a novice. Once I move abroad I'll be out of sight and out of mind! So bollocks to it!' Darren stood up and headed for the bar.

'God, he could be hard work,' Nick thought. Claire stared at him stonily. He gave her a plaintive gesture.

'Most players would get down on bended Armanis for the chance to play in Italy! You've lived abroad, haven't you? Tell him how good it can be!'

Claire said nothing, leaving Nick to fear that the deal would go down. If Darren settled for staying put on a peanuts wage-rate, Nick would be off. Agents could have no time for losers.

All in the Game

**Gary Lineker
with Stan Hey**

CORONET BOOKS
Hodder and Stoughton

British Library CIP

A CIP catalogue record for this title is available from the British Library

ISBN 0-340-60747-5

10 9 8 7 6 5 4 3 2 1

Printed and bound in Great Britain for Hodder and Stoughton Paperbacks, a division of Hodder and Stoughton Ltd, Mill Road, Dunton Green, Sevenoaks, Kent TN13 2YA (Editorial Office: 47 Bedford Square, London WC1B 3DP) by Cox and Wyman Ltd, Reading. Photoset by Rowland Phototypesetting Ltd, Bury St Edmunds, Suffolk.

Chapter One

Darren reckoned it was the best goal he'd scored for a long while. A nice early cross from the right wing which left defenders ball-watching, while he was able to get a run in front of the centre-half and, wallop! – the ball thumped off the dead-centre of his forehead into the bottom corner of the net. Nice way to complete a hat-trick.

Without even thinking Darren ran to the crowd behind the goal, his right index finger raised to let them know who was Number One. He'd got this idea from his dad, who'd organised all those sessions in the back garden after school which were now, albeit sixteen years later, bearing fruit. Target practice against an old sheet of hardboard, which had the shape of a goal whitewashed on it, and numbered squares, 1 to 5 – the further from the 'goalkeeper's' reach, the higher the number. This evening's goal had been a definite 'five'.

'There's Only One Darren Matthews!' the home crowd chanted, and another section followed up with 'Darren For England!' Darren claimed the match ball off the ref at the end of the game, the fourth time he'd collared this traditional trophy for hat-tricks that season. After years of promise – and a couple of under achievement, it had to be said – Darren was finally up there with the best centre-forwards in the Premier League.

1

So the gaggle of press-men waiting in the corridor outside the dressing-room only wanted to talk to one person. Darren would come up with some much-needed 'nannies' (nanny-goats – quotes) for the next morning's papers, even if he did have to be force-fed with the usual gambit 'Would you say that . . . ?', which prefaced all their questions: '. . . you can catch Kenny Dawes's team?' . . . 'you're now hoping for an England call-up?' . . . 'you're in a position to look for a new, improved contract from the club?'

The answer to all these questions was basically 'yes', but Darren was too pumped-up after the match to deal in those monosyllabic exchanges which had too often been associated with footballers.

'I think we can push Dawes's team all the way to the wire,' he asserted confidently, 'especially if we can get a couple of players before the transfer deadline.'

It was the adrenalin talking. The sheer spill-over of the excitement that he had generated in the crowd with his goals, and which they'd transmitted back to him with their acclaim. Darren knew too what the club's sustained challenge in the Premier League had done for the town. He was a local boy, had stood on the terraces with his dad watching the club drifting between the old First and Second Divisions without ever achieving anything. Now they had a chance to put one over the high-spending, big city clubs which were threatening to dominate the English game – and it was his goal-scoring that was fuelling that belief.

The atmosphere in Alfredo's Italian restaurant, Darren's usual post-match haunt, reflected the ebullience of the town. Diners came over and shook him by the hand. Alfredo kept pointing out the signed photo of Darren which hung on the wall alongside the other star players he'd have liked to have had as customers – Baggio, Lentini, Vialli and yes, even Gascoigne. And

Nick Young, Darren's agent and business manager who'd come up from London for the night, was in pursuit of a fat Havana cigar to celebrate. His excitement, though, had already been processed into more practical terms.

'Now then, Darren, I think tonight's a good time to talk about your new contract,' he said, tilting back his head so that he could blow the cigar smoke up from the table.

Darren shifted uneasily. Deals and money-talk bored him at the best of times, a characteristic which Nick had attributed to the smothering feudalism which most young footballers had to deal with when they turned professional. It had always been in the interest of football clubs to bamboozle players about money early in their careers. The less they knew, the less they expected. This was Nick's analysis, but then, as an agent, he would think that, wouldn't he?

Nick had made an appointment the following day for the two of them to go in and see the club's chairman and chief executive, Derek Horsfield. Darren's three goals, and the press momentum for his call-up to the England squad, had put them in a very strong position to demand a much-improved contract from Horsfield. 'Position of Maximum Opportunity', Nick called it, borrowing the phrase used by an old soccer guru from the fifties.

Darren put up a rearguard action, both in the restaurant and when they adjourned to his flat. It wasn't just that he preferred to play Simply Red as loud as possible on the stereo, or to have a laugh and a few more glasses of wine. The real problem was that his girlfriend Claire was with them, and Darren just hated, in fact couldn't even bring himself, to talk money in front of her.

To anyone from another table, Claire looked like a

classic footballer's companion. Shoulder-length blonde hair, pretty face, slim and fashionably dressed. You'd have guessed at an IQ in the low thirties, an affection for fluffy toys and an ambition to be the weather-girl on the local news.

But Claire Travis was not like this. For a start, the clothes she wore had been designed by herself. She'd studied fashion – and the business side of it – at Art College. She'd schlepped around Paris with her portfolio for a year, picking up contacts, ideas and a few disreputable boyfriends.

And when she'd started her relationship with Darren two years previously, she'd accepted his kind offer of support – it actually translated into a £3,000 cheque in an envelope on the breakfast table – and opened up her own shop in the Victorian part of the town centre.

So part of Darren's reluctance to 'get fiscal' with Claire was simply down to him knowing that she knew more about it than he did. Claire thought she knew another reason, and told him so when he eventually slid into bed beside her, hoping for a belated fuck to complete the winding-down process.

'If you'd sorted out your business at the restaurant, there'd have been time for this,' Claire spluttered. 'Your mother's told me! Married over twenty-seven years and she still isn't allowed to know how much your dad earns! It must be hereditary!'

Darren rolled on his back. 'The reason I didn't want to talk about the deal in front of you was because I didn't want you to get *bored*!' He put a tentative hand on her upper thigh.

'Piss off, Darren!'

Claire brushed him off again. Darren had been attracted to Claire because she was different from the usual run of girls footballers met. Claire had hoped that

4

Darren could be different too. She'd taken a lot of stick from her 'arty' friends for going out with someone they considered naff, despite his money.

To a great extent the relationship had succeeded – an executive-style home on a rurally named inner-city site was nearing completion. Tonight apart, they had an energetic sex-life. An informal engagement had been announced, and marriage was on the cards. But at times like this, lying in the dark after a row, both Claire and Darren felt the absence of the kind of partners that their previous lives had led them to expect – an open, mature, adventurous type for her, and a compliant, no-questions-asked bimbo for him.

Derek Horsfield's evening hadn't gone too well either. On the face of it a good home win, the three points which maintained the club's championship challenge, and a decent take at the gate should have been an excuse for any chief executive to have a few drinks in the directors' lounge after the match. The problem was that he found himself being out-drunk by the club's bank manager, who didn't look like he was in a celebratory mood.

'Want a lift in the Securicor van so you can check the takings?' Horsfield asked, trying to cajole a laugh out of Ed the bank manager. Ed, propped up on a red leatherette stool, clung to the bar as if it was a life-raft. He glowered at Horsfield.

'Don't you regard it as worrying to see me getting pissed out of my skull?'

'I thought you were having a good time. The bank that likes to say "yesh"!' Horsfield offered.

Ed looked balefully around the room to check that he and Horsfield were alone.

'London have been on. They want an immediate

reduction in borrowing. If not, they'll send up some real ball-crusher to do it for you!'

Horsfield felt suddenly sober, despite the burn of another brandy in his windpipe. He shrugged weakly at Ed.

'We've been making economies . . .'

Ed snapped. 'Make some bloody money, Derek! *Quick!* Sell some flesh. That thing scoring the goals tonight. Must be worth a few bob?'

'Darren?' Horsfield stammered, shocked at the intensity of Ed's behaviour. 'He's priceless!'

'Nothing's priceless,' Ed barked as he clambered gracelessly off the stool and made his way unsteadily towards the toilets. 'So get rid. Get rid!'

Slumped in the back of his chauffeur-driven Rolls-Royce, Horsfield stared out at the late-night burger bars and kebab-houses which peppered the route from the ground to his home outside the city. He envied their simplicity sometimes, especially after a night like this. Low overheads. Cash payments. Flexible hours. If only football clubs could be run like that. But they couldn't, of course.

Success bred not success but costs as far as Horsfield was concerned – converting the ground to an all-seater stadium hadn't seen much change out of £6 million despite grants from the Football Trust; and of course the wage bills went up constantly. You had to pay up or risk breaking up the team, which in turn risked pushing you back down the spiral into poverty again. Players, and yes their bastard agents, were always trying to score more money.

So Darren and Nick Young were not exactly welcome when they came in the following morning to sort out Darren's contract which was about to expire at the end of the season.

Horsfield tried to lighten the atmosphere by trying

to off-load some two-tone shirts which a club Vice-President had 'donated' to the players in the hope of attracting some cheap publicity.

'Naff,' said Nick Young, tossing the shirt back, without noticing that Horsfield was wearing one of the same batch. One–nil to the visitors.

Horsfield retaliated by sliding his chair over to what he hoped would be viewed as his 'work-station' – in fact a second-hand Amstrad – and busily clicked away at the keyboard. He made a great play of examining the flickering screen before swivelling back to Darren and Nick Young.

'The crystal ball says that all I can offer you, Darren, is an increase of half-a-K per week on basic.'

Young laughed – not briefly, but lengthily and loudly.

'Are you sure you haven't just called up some youth team player with the same surname as Darren?'

Horsfield twitched with anger.

'Do you find an extra "monkey" a week to be a laughing matter, Darren?'

Darren shifted uneasily. He didn't like talking about money in front of Horsfield either. Making his career with his home-town club had left him with the ever-so-slightly naïve attitude that they wouldn't rip off a local lad.

'Don't ask me to say what I think I'm worth,' Darren said with a nervous smile.

Horsfield didn't quite buy this shrinking-violet line. He showed Darren the back page of that morning's *Daily Star*, which carried the headline 'Help Me, Begs Hat-Trick Star Darren'. The previous evening's casual observation about the club buying a couple more players had been reprocessed by the tabloid's sports-desk into an eye-catching story. Darren still had a lot to learn about the ways of the press.

'You seem to have strong opinions about the club's

7

transfer policy,' Horsfield said sarkily. 'I've already had two managers on this morning trying to unload players onto us! Little do they know!'

The knockabout stuff had finished now. The real, hard-edge negotiating began, with Horsfield and Nick Young trading their estimates of Darren's worth as though he wasn't in the room. A market auction would have had more dignity. When Nick played his ace card – the threat of looking for a move elsewhere – Horsfield blew his stack.

'How dare you hold a bloody gun to my head! I wish you knew what I was up against. There are forces out there that I can't control!'

This sounded like hysterical nonsense to Nick, who quickly suggested a few days' adjournment to allow tempers to cool and Horsfield to come up with a better offer.

Darren was churned up by the row, and by Nick's apparent belief that it had been 'good for openers'. The aggressive confidence which footballers displayed on the pitch often dissolved into a twitchy paranoia off it. 'Why are they being like this? How could they value me so lowly? Do they want to get rid of me?' were just three of the questions pinging around inside Darren's head.

But that was nothing compared to what Horsfield was going through. It felt like the bank manager had attached jump-leads to his vital parts, and that Darren and Nick Young had been switching the current on and off. Horsfield desperately wanted to hang on to Darren – he was the club's one star. But he couldn't push through a big hike in wages in the circumstances. 'Get rid, get rid', he kept hearing as he paced his office trying to work out his next move.

Ten minutes later he'd resolved it – a fellow club chairman had tipped him off about a guy called Sandor

Kosics, a former Hungarian international, who'd now become a big 'fixer' on the European transfer market. If Darren was going to leave the club, Horsfield wanted the best price – and that meant Europe.

He called Kosics's office in Zurich and was pleased to find that the Hungarian spoke good English, and had also heard of Darren's scoring exploits. When Horsfield's secretary burst into the office to tell him that the England manager was on the line for him, Horsfield's brain began to swirl and his hands began to twitch. The electric current had been switched on again.

The news of Darren Matthews's call-up to the England squad upped the stakes all round. Horsfield suddenly had something more elevated to sell than a run-of-the-mill centre-forward. Nick Young had a higher brand of product to market and Darren had a new future ahead of him.

He whisked Claire off from her shop and took her out to where their house was being built. The kitchen-fitters had gone off for lunch leaving the still-unpacked units piled around the main living space. Yet it was a good place to break his news about England, because it symbolised the future that he and Claire were seemingly stumbling towards.

Darren strategically placed the word 'we' into a reference to the house and waited tentatively for Claire to react.

'Are you saying that you still want me to come and live with you,' she asked, sympathetically.

Darren gestured around him. 'It's a bit big for one, isn't it?'

Claire began to circle the room, trying to imagine life there, with Darren, England's new centre-forward, while she busied herself with her design work and shop. All in all, it felt right. Her smile confirmed that to Darren who was watching her intently. Claire recognised the look.

'Do you fancy christening the kitchen, then?' she smirked as she moved towards him, and started to undo the buttons on his shirt.

Darren shivered at the touch of her lips on his chest. His hands stroked her hips, pulling her closer to him. Then he laughed.

'What?' Claire asked with a frown.

'I'm just trying to imagine how I'm going to keep a straight face when some journalist asks me how I celebrated the news.'

'Simple,' said Claire, resuming her kissing. 'Tell them you defrosted the fridge . . .'

Claire backed Darren up against one of the boxes as she locked her mouth onto his. They pirouetted around the appliances, shedding clothes before Claire stretched out and invited Darren to make up for the time they'd lost last night.

Meanwhile, Horsfield was down at the bank, getting a hung-over Ed to stack thirty grand in cash into his attaché case.

'Is this for one of them . . . what do you call it . . . *bungs*?' Ed asked blearily.

Horsfield wagged an index finger.

'Careful . . . you don't want to know about things like that. Let's just say that a transfer is like launching a ship – you have to grease the slipway.'

The earth moved for both Darren and Claire that lunchtime but what they didn't know was where it was going to stop.

It was fully fifteen hours before Darren could catch up with his father to celebrate the England call-up, and even then it involved Darren rising at 5.30 a.m. to catch his dad as he finished work. Freddie Matthews, a burly

10

forty-six-year-old, humped carcasses at the town's meat-market, clocking-on around ten every night and working his way through to a pie and a pint breakfast at 6.30 the next morning.

Freddie'd specifically asked Darren to get there before he finished, a transparent attempt to milk the applause of the other porters, butchers and buyers who shared this bizarre night-life.

Sure enough Darren got the full range of compliments from 'the boys' as he made his way past the huge, humming refrigerated lorries and into the market hall itself, which was ablaze with the harsh light of thousands of bare bulbs.

Darren smiled and waved modestly. He'd known a lot of the faces for years, and a couple even belonged to people he'd been at school with. Creased with lines of stress and sleeplessness, the faces, even with smiles, took on a surreal quality in the stark, bluish light. They almost adopted the colouring of the dead meat that hung all around them. Darren knew that there'd be times up ahead when the public would want to stick the knife into him, but he also knew that here were people who would always support him because they were individually touched and enriched by his 'fame'. That Darren had 'got out' was a source of celebration, not resentment.

Freddie made a great play of wiping his hands on his stained white overalls before clasping Darren.

'Who's my little super-star then?'

Darren backed away, jokingly defending his dark-blue, Paul Smith suit. 'Mind the clothes! Don't want giblets all over me!'

Freddie looked him in the eye.

'I'm really chuffed, son! For you more than for me!'

Darren nodded and smiled. Cheers went up around them.

'Come on, I'll take you for a pint,' said Freddie as he began to peel off his overalls.

'Dad, I'm training in three hours!'

With the public ritual over, Freddie and Darren settled into a corner of the local pub which opened early to provide some cheer for the market workers. The occasional white-collar type, driving in from the suburbs, would drop by for a fry-up breakfast and a dusting of street credibility. But this morning it was just the lads from the market, who drooled over the tabloid back pages, all of which led on Darren's elevation to the big-time.

'I still can't get over it – *my* son, playing for England!' Freddie said after he'd sipped through the froth on his first pint. 'Mind you, I always knew you would. You were born to it!'

'The only thing I appear to have inherited from you is a reluctance to talk money in front of women,' Darren retaliated wryly.

Freddie chuckled to himself.

'That would be the *second* thing I taught you!'

Freddie reminded Darren, not that he needed it, of the target range he'd built for his son in the back garden of their council house. He was, understandably, claiming his share of the credit for Darren's success, not in a spirit of self-glorification, more a sense of shared nostalgia.

'Anyway, all I did was to try and finish off what nature had started.'

Now this *did* rankle. Darren knew his strengths, and natural talent hadn't been one of them. He was a self-made footballer. Hard work, on the practice pitch and in matches themselves, had been the source of his achievements. He'd learned the game as he went along, slowly discovering what worked for him. And the last couple of years with Claire, who'd been both a no-

12

nonsense critic and an inspirational supporter, had helped him focus on what he did best – score goals.

'It's been nothing to do with destiny, Dad,' Darren said, his tone sharpened by the disruption of the early rise.

'Oh, no?' asked Freddie confidently. He took another swig of his pint and wiped his lips with the relish of somebody about to reveal a deep secret. 'I want you to go back nine months from when you were born . . .'

Reluctantly, Darren played along and counted back. 'August 1966. So what?'

'Try late July,' said Freddie with a smirk. 'Saturday the 30th, to be precise!' He followed up with a few suggestive winks. 'England 4 – West Germany 2. Does that help you a little?'

Darren gawped at him, unable to take in the sheer daftness of what Freddie was proposing.

'What are you trying to say? That because I *might* have been conceived the day England won the World Cup, I was destined to play for my country? Get off!'

'If you don't believe me, ask your mother how we celebrated!'

Darren shook his head. Parents retained memories of all kinds of little childhood moments to embarrass you in later life – when you crapped on the neighbour's carpet, when you swore for the first time in front of the vicar, when you were caught playing with yourself. But this seemed a bizarre delusion. Darren quickly tried to puncture it.

'Well, if you're right, I suppose I've got West Germany in 1970 to blame for the fact that I'm an only child!'

Freddie smiled at the joke, but his face said he was sticking to his story. Darren shrugged in defeat, but couldn't let him go without a warning of the dreaded consequences if Freddie ever blabbed this belief to a tabloid journalist.

'Don't ever tell 'em. They'd make my life a bloody misery. You know what they're like. They'd be conducting polls on how many people had it away the night England won! They'd . . . they'd be encouraging couples to breed a new super-race of footballers and cricketers. So just leave it alone, eh, Dad?'

Freddie shrugged and finished his drink, perhaps sensing for the first time how much was at stake for Darren now. He shivered briefly at the thought of it all becoming too serious.

'Well, it's a pity. I bet they could have had some fun with World Cup Willie!'

Darren knew this was true – he could see the front page of the *Sun* with the 1966 World Cup mascot urging a bonk-in for England. He couldn't help laughing at the thought. But it would be the only laugh for the next few weeks.

Sure the rest of the team had a few jovial digs in training about the new England star in their midst, all of which Darren rode out. But it was the call he took from Nick Young on his portable phone after training which brought the clouds down on the day.

'Horsfield's sticking at a five hundred a week rise, final offer . . .' Nick told him.

Darren couldn't really talk in the dressing-room, nor could he allow his face to give anything away. Especially as the team manager Ray Peters was hovering, giving out his Brownie points for the morning's work.

So Darren could only mumble a few 'yes', 'no', 'right' expressions down the phone as he listened with dismay to Nick's determination to 'put the frighteners on Horsfield in a big way'. What this would involve, God only knew. Darren certainly didn't want to think about it.

But with the rest of the squad gone by the time he'd

14

finished his call, there were none of the usual distrac-
tions – a game of snooker, an afternoon at the races,
a pub lunch, or a round of golf – available to him.

So he drifted down to Claire's shop in the hope that
he could entice her out for half an hour. A repeat of the
previous day's exertions in the half-completed kitchen
would be too much to hope for. But she had other
ways of lifting him out of his occasional descents into
depression, not the least of which was the rationality
of someone outside the game.

Unfortunately, Claire was in her office at the back
of the shop, dealing with a trade-buyer. Her part-time
assistant, Jane, stood guard, and couldn't help but
enjoy the moment that Darren's arrival and Claire's
absence had given her.

'Do you want a cup of coffee while you wait?' she
offered.

Darren hovered uneasily just inside the door, like a
customer who'd suddenly realised he'd left his wallet
at home.

'I'll, er, go and do a bit of shopping, I think. Haven't
bought a jacket for at least a week.'

The joke was a mistake, and he knew it the moment
Jane laughed at it. He could sense her presumption of
intimacy. Darren tried to back away.

'No . . . *yeah*. Say I'll see her back at the flat later.'

'Hers or yours?' Jane probed.

'Mine, I guess.'

Jane moved a step closer. 'I hear you're moving in
together?'

'Probably.'

Jane looked over her shoulder to check that Claire
was still tucked away in the office. Even though she
was, Jane still lowered her voice.

'I hope we'll still be able to see something of each
other.'

Darren tried another joke to lighten the atmosphere.

'If I keep hanging round women's clothes shops people will begin to talk.' It didn't work.

'You know what I mean. I'm in tonight if you want to pop round.'

Darren cursed himself for taking the risk of coming down to the shop. With his gaze fixed on Claire sitting talking in her office, he tried as firmly as he could to let Jane know the score.

'Look, Jane. I think we should knock it on the head. Been a bit of fun while it's lasted. But it's not easy. For either of us.'

Jane smiled confidently at him. This time the intimacy was no presumption.

'You'll be round. I know what you like.'

'Maybe my tastes are changing,' was the best he could come up with in the circumstances. He backed away and left.

The affair with Jane had started six months ago, though 'affair' was dignifying it somewhat. He'd run her back to her poky little flat one night – ironically as a favour to Claire – only to find himself invited in and then jumped on. Darren wasn't entirely innocent, of course. He hadn't declined Jane's baldly stated desire to go down on him. The sheer sensual thrill of watching her red lips and painted finger-nails at work on him was worth the risk. Or so it seemed at the time.

Sporadic bouts of sheer naughtiness had followed, usually involving kitchen tables, shower cubicles and Jane in a variety of exotic underwear. Darren thought he'd worked through all that with Claire in the early months of their relationship. Gradually, the fripperies and novelty locations had been supplanted by a mature intensity that needed no window-dressing. So he'd been shocked at his own vulnerability to Jane's approach.

The footballer's usual rationale – that this sort of

thing was just no-nonsense shagging, a minor fringe benefit of local fame, to be enjoyed for what it was – had held good for a while. So too had the cowardly assertion that he had a right to experiment further before taking marriage vows with Claire. But gradually Darren had felt himself ill at ease with the double-life. It wasn't just the papers and the television banging on about the risk of AIDS among heterosexuals that had got to him. He genuinely wanted to clean up his act and settle down with Claire.

As he retreated to his BMW, Darren just hoped that Jane had got the latest message. The thought of what might happen if she ever told Claire dogged him throughout the rest of the afternoon. At going on twenty-six, Darren had decided he wanted to keep life simple: a big new home, with a wife and a few kids to follow, and the completion of his career with the one club – England appearances excepted! – seemed a pretty good package compared to his dad's life down at the meat market. 'I'd settle for that,' Darren thought as he flipped through the racing results on Teletext.

Chapter Two

'They're messing Darren around something rotten. Horsfield's stalling on a new contract.' Nick Young made his opening pitch then leaned back to watch the reaction of his lunch-guest.

Opposite him, Kenny Dawes was affecting a look of complete indifference. Correction. It wasn't affected, but entirely genuine. As manager of the team currently leading the English Premier League – and most experts reckoned they'd soon be champions – he had about as much interest in Darren Matthews's contractual troubles as Salman Rushdie would have in a new picnic basket.

'So?' asked Dawes, shrugging expressively in the hope that Nick would register his interest level. Nick didn't.

'Well – would you be interested in buying Darren? If you win the title you'll have three or four million quid to spend!' Nick beamed, pleased with his solution to Darren's wages dispute.

Dawes quite liked Nick Young – well, make that he didn't mind him too much. Among the increasingly rag-bag array of half-wits and opportunists who purported to be football agents, Nick stood out like a beacon of integrity and intelligence. That's how bad the rest of them seemed to Kenny Dawes. Even so, Dawes didn't like being hustled into transfers. He still liked to think of himself as a lone prowler, striking when he wanted to, not when some player's agent suggested.

He was still trying to frame a polite reply in his mind when an overly made-up waitress in a St Trinian's boater, short skirt and stockings, interrupted them, her pencil poised over her red school exercise-book which doubled as an order pad. The place had been a favourite haunt since it had opened in the mid-eighties, and Kenny was glad he'd suggested it for their lunch venue, since it had lost none of what he saw as its exuberant tackiness. Indeed he saw it as a metaphor for his own survival against the forces of decorum and dignity in football. Not that Kenny knew precisely what a metaphor was.

'Right, you naughty boys. I'm ready to take down what you want,' leered the waitress. 'Cook says the salmon's the business today . . .'

Dawes checked the menu to find that a portion of the fish would haul in twenty-five quid's worth of business.

'Got its own agent, has it?' he asked with a wink at Nick.

'Your friend's going to get a smacked botty if he's cheeky,' the waitress slurped to Nick, who looked the more responsible of the two, primarily because he wore glasses.

'Two salmon then. And another Moët.' Dawes tapped the neck of the first bottle which rested in an ice-bucket by the table. Might as well enjoy myself, he'd thought after accepting Nick's invitation.

The waitress wandered away, carrying Dawes's gaze with her.

Nick tried to win back his attention.

'Come on, you'll need goals to succeed in Europe. And Darren gets them.'

Dawes snapped out of his libidinous thoughts. '*This*

20

season . . . look, Nick, the simple truth is, I don't rate him.'

Nick tried to keep his defiant expression together. Belief in a client's abilities went with the job, and Darren's recent surge of success had inured him even to the *possibility* of adverse criticism. This felt like a slap in the face.

'I can see that your demands are met . . .' he retaliated.

'What demands would that be?' Dawes asked stonily.

Nick leant forward, hissing at him. 'Come on – you're infamous, Kenny! I know what you'd expect off the top of any transfer deal . . .'

Dawes assumed a face of perfect innocence.

'I really can't imagine what you're talking about, Nick.'

Nick's eyes widened in desperation. He'd really thought that Dawes would take the bait in the first instance.

'You and I could stitch up Horsfield a treat! I could get you twenty . . . thirty grand!'

Dawes held up his podgy right hand, festooned with two gold sovereign rings.

'Nick, I don't buy players I don't fancy! *Whatever's* on offer! Now look, I'll do you a favour. I'll plant a story in the *Mirror* that I'm coming in for Darren – the supporters'll go bonkers, Horsfield'll shit himself and then Darren will get his new contract.'

Nick's face registered defeat for the first time.

'Okay, if that's the best I can get.'

'But you'll owe me one, right?'

Nick nodded, wishing now that he'd never phoned, and dreading the thought of a further hour in Dawes's company. Swamped by disappointment, he only half heard Dawes's side of the tawdry bargain.

'Starting now . . . I'd like you to do a bit of name-dropping to help me pull this trollop!' Dawes flashed a would-be cheeky smile as the waitress returned with the next bottle of champagne.

Nick scrambled for a suitable gambit as the nail-bitten fingers tore at the foil on the top of the bottle.

'Er . . . do you like football, miss?'

The continuing dead-lock over his contract, and the nagging worry about how to fend off Jane, fogged Darren's mind for several days. He even struggled to raise a smile when Ted Yale, the editor of the club's programme, called round to conduct a questionnaire on Darren's 'favourite things'. Most of the lads enjoyed this, seizing the chance to take the piss out of what they saw as the 'train-spotting' element among the fans, which Ted more or less personified.

None of them had ever risen to the heights achieved by that flamboyant 1970s centre-forward Frank Worthington who'd replied to the question 'Who's been your toughest opponent in football?' with 'My ex-wife.' But that wouldn't stop them trying.

Today, though, Darren was too deflated to deal with anything other than mundanity.

'Favourite food?' Yale asked, his cheap, leaking ballpoint poised over his notepad.

'Lasagne,' said Darren, who then checked himself. 'No, that sounds a bit posey. Make it liver and bacon.'

Yale laboriously corrected the entry on the form as Darren watched the hands of the clock go backwards.

'Music?'

Darren shrugged. 'Soul.' Seeing the blank look on Yale's face he expanded a little. 'Simply Red, Alexander O'Neal, Luther Vandross, old Motown, that sort of thing.'

This was the bit Ted Yale hated most. The bit where

he realised how out of touch he was. He'd rarely heard of any of the players' favourite singers and, in the absence of a surprise nomination for Pearl Carr and Teddy Johnson or Frankie Laine, always had to check the spellings with his grandson later. 'Luther Van Dross? Must be a Dutchman,' he thought.

'Right, last one – favourite moment in football.'

Darren thought. None of his own achievements seemed to be worth recording in print. The odd spectacular goal, the hat-tricks, the couple of away wins at Anfield or Old Trafford. Was that it? He'd never actually *won* anything. Hearing the news of his England call-up would be a bit obvious. Besides, it was tempting fate. He hadn't got in the national team yet. Now, that *would* be a moment.

Then from out of the furthest corner of his mind, prompted no doubt by his sombre mood, came a genuinely spine-tingling memory.

'It was a European Cup semi-final, a few days after Hillsborough. AC Milan versus Real Madrid. The ref stopped the game for a minute's silence and after it the Italian fans sang "You'll Never Walk Alone". I thought that was brilliant.'

Yale looked at him and saw the momentary glistening in Darren's eyes. The whole football world had been touched by the Hillsborough Stadium disaster. Reforms had come out of it. But so too had a new attitude by the players to the fans who paid their wages. Ted thought it was nice that Darren had acknowledged that.

'Right, thanks, much appreciated,' Ted said as he folded his pad.

'I'm glad someone at the club does – appreciate me, that is,' Darren prompted.

Yale didn't like getting involved in club politics. But he liked Darren a lot. Most of the club's ordinary workers and supporters did; he was still 'one of them'.

'My spies tell me you're having a bit of a ruck with Horsfield.'

Darren shrugged.

'He's only doing his job. One thing, Ted. Don't let it get around that I'm being a greedy bastard, 'cos I'm not.'

Yale smiled at him.

'I know, son. We all think the world of you here.'

Darren was momentarily touched by this testimony. But then Ted Yale didn't have to sort out the wages bill. His mood continued to be sour throughout the rest of the day, and certainly wasn't helped by Claire eagerly sifting through a clutch of holiday brochures she'd brought home.

In technical terms, her timing was right – the football season had just over four weeks to run – but in terms of tact, she was way off the mark. The close season is a time of upheaval for any player who is on the move or falling out of contract. And anyone who'd also been called up for the England squad's summer programme of games could throw his diary right out of the window. Darren had at least two of these preoccupations on his mind, so his input for the holiday discussion over dinner had consisted largely of a series of grunts.

Claire had backed off, sensing a deeper malaise. But when she saw Darren have a complete shit-fit over one of her brochures sticking to the bottom of his coffee-mug, she had to ask or risk dying of imploded laughter.

'This isn't just the usual holidays tantrum, is it?'

Darren stalked the large open-plan room, looking for a coaster on which he could place his mug.

'Don't get a strop on, Claire, it's the last thing I need after the last few days . . .'

As the requested silence fell, Claire tried to work out whether she was supposed to take up the all too obvious sub-text of him not having a good time. Noting a dash of self-pity in the tone, she risked the enquiry, but was damned if she was going to make it sympathetically.

'That's all the explanation I'm getting, is it?'

Darren put an end to his prowling and slumped onto one of the leather sofas which framed the coffee-table. He sighed heavily, and then, without looking Claire directly in the eye, proceeded to run down the precise difficulties he was experiencing with Horsfield and the club. He even told her how much he, well, Nick to be accurate, was asking for on the new contract. Claire said nothing about this breakthrough in their relationship, sensing Darren's genuine confusion. Now he looked at her.

'Go on, tell me I'm out of touch with the real world. Not worth it.'

'Not at all. Without your goals, where would the team be?'

Claire's quick response surprised Darren. And he knew it was genuine because she'd never got into the business of flattering him. He gave her a smile of acknowledgement.

'You've got to decide what *you* want, Darren – then tell Nick, and tell the club!'

The forceful simplicity of Claire's thinking cheered him up.

'I just want to play football. To win. And the team means everything to me. I hate it when anything gets in the way of that.'

In bed, watching Claire sleeping next to him, it occurred to Darren that he was equally disturbed by the possibility that Jane might come between him and Claire. He reassured himself that nothing could have been said that afternoon, and with this optimistic omen lodged in his brain, he fell asleep hoping for a better tomorrow.

Within seconds of being woken the next morning by

25

Claire, the light admitted by the opened curtains seemed to have turned to gloom. Claire had thrust the back page of the *Daily Mirror* under his face.

'Somebody's been playing silly buggers . . .'

The headline for the lead story read: 'Dawes Open for Darren?', the gist of the story being simply that Kenny Dawes was about to make an offer for Darren's services.

Darren was straight onto the phone to Nick, finding the one-way conversation he'd intended greatly assisted by the fact that Nick was eating a jam doughnut for breakfast.

'I don't need stunts like this, Nick! It doesn't look good when the moment I get into the England set-up I'm suddenly spread over the back pages! It's pressure. And you're supposed to take that off me. Now kill the story! *Quick!*'

The damage had been done, however. As Darren drove into the training ground, the team manager stood on the steps of the pavilion glowering at him. Darren tried to dodge past him into the changing-rooms, but he could tell Peters was spoiling for a fight.

'Not good enough for you now, are we?'

Darren turned wearily. 'It's paper talk, boss. I know nothing about it . . .'

Darren went to move away only to find Peters's arm across his chest, holding him back.

'I turn a blind eye to one story telling me you think I should buy more players . . .'

'. . . I was misquoted, boss . . .'

'Next day you're England's new saviour and now you're touting yourself round the transfer market!'

Darren looked at Peters fiercely. He could see how it all looked if you strung three back pages together, but Peters didn't have to believe them unless he wanted to.

'That's not the way it is! Not on my side anyway.'

Peters moved round in front of him, flexing a shoulder muscle.

'What's that supposed to mean? *What?*'

Darren eye-balled him, fighting back with some rumour-mongering of his own.

'Well, maybe you're looking at me and thinking you could get three new lads if I was flogged off!'

'Where did you get this crap from?' Peters asked, seeming genuinely bemused.

'Let's just say it's a spin-off from trying to get a decent contract out of the chairman of this club.'

'Wait a minute, wait a minute – *he* tells me you've been trying it on, Darren. That's the cause of all the trouble.'

Darren shook his head in bitter exasperation. All he'd done was ask for a pay-rise, now the whole club seemed to have a down on him.

'Why, Darren? After all the work I've put into you. Two years ago I had to stop Horsfield bumming you out on a free transfer. Now you're Mr Big Head. Well let me tell you, if you shit on me, son, I'll gladly pay somebody above the going rate to break both your legs!'

Darren broke violently free of Peters's grip.

'Nice to know you value me so highly, boss!'

Darren stalked off into the pavilion, convinced more than ever that he and Nick had been set up by Horsfield and that anything they did in retaliation would play into his hands.

By Saturday, relations between Darren and the club had deteriorated further. There'd been no comeback from Horsfield at all, which wasn't really surprising, given that he had now formally 'commissioned' Sandor Kosics at a secret Heathrow meeting to 'take a little piggy to market', the piggy being Darren, the market

27

being any of the top clubs in Europe. Neither Darren nor Nick was aware of this of course. Nor was Nick up to speed on the latest development between Peters and Darren as he arrived in the marble-clad lobby at Arsenal for that afternoon's game. Darren was waiting there ready to hand over Nick's guest ticket, the equivalent of a back-stage pass, which would admit Nick to the world of suits and wheeler-dealers in the directors' lounge.

'Bit late getting changed, aren't you?' he observed, checking his watch.

Darren flashed a sardonic smile.

'I've been dropped. The boss thinks I should be out of the team till I get my head sorted out.'

Nick was almost lost for words.

'But that's . . .'

'*Your* fault . . . yeah. So, I don't want you steaming in up there to sort things out! Monday morning, I'm going in and accepting Horsfield's original offer. Get all this behind me.'

Nick bristled. This was not just a defeat, but an insult to the work he'd done.

'You do that and you can kiss goodbye to our association!'

Darren nodded. 'Oh, good – a bonus!'

Nick looked around to check the likelihood of any eavesdroppers before leaning in close to Darren's face.

'Listen, you little prick! You've got maybe five, six more years in this game and then you're a nobody! You make your money *now*, because it won't be there then! You'll be licking journalists' arses for fifty quid a throw. I've seen 'em. All the old wrecks who whinge on about how little they got out of the game because there was nobody to fight their corner!'

Darren appeared unmoved. 'I can look after myself, thanks.' And he headed off through the door bearing

28

the sign 'Players Only' – an inner sanctum, a retreat, the only world he really knew.

Stuck in the back of the team dug-out for the match, Darren had to suffer not only the isolation of the player suddenly discarded from relevant action, he also had to suppress the mounting sense of perverse relish as the team fell a goal behind. At the final whistle, they'd lost 2–0, severely denting their championship hopes. Darren felt for the lads, the chasm of disappointment at seeing so much effort dribbling away. But he couldn't quell the urge to gloat over the fact that Peters's disciplinary measure had back-fired so spectacularly.

Darren tried hard to explain this conflict of emotions to Claire that night as he sought refuge from press enquiries and public scrutiny at his flat.

'Can't you see? I'm gutted! I sat on that bench this afternoon just *dying* to see my own team get beat! The club I've supported since I was a kid. Can you imagine how bad that feels?'

Claire was plainly irritated by his reaction. For her, the issue was cut and dried.

'*Bad?* They drop you, and then they lose *because* they dropped you! I'm surprised you didn't do cartwheels along the touchline!'

Darren wasn't really listening. His eyes had gone dead. He stared at nothing in particular.

'I feel like I'm going mad. I was walking on air three days ago. Now *this*! I'm out of the team, I have a bust-up with the boss, I have a bust-up with Nick.'

Claire took the opportunity to let rip.

'Well, he's no loss, is he? Manipulative sod does more in *his* interests than yours . . .'

Before Darren could respond the phone rang. He shrugged at Claire.

'Probably be some shit-stirring journalist. I'm not in.'

Claire dutifully crossed the room and answered the

phone. But her normally efficient defensive shield faltered this time as a frown crossed her face. Darren registered her change of tone as she held the receiver out for him.

'Somebody called Sandor Kosy or something. Phoning from Zurich . . .'

Darren looked utterly confused. The name meant nothing. But in his present frame of mind, he sensed only trouble. He took hold of the phone reluctantly, and found a confident, foreign voice telling him what was about to happen to his career.

'You what?' Darren spluttered. 'Wait a minute – I don't know how you got my number, mate, but . . . that's what you say . . . Look, I'm not in the mood for practical jokes, so piss off, eh?'

Darren slammed the receiver down then took it off and let it lie on the floor.

'Who was it?' Claire asked seeing the confusion it had caused Darren.

'Some bloody fruitcake trying to tell me that Sampdoria in Italy are about to buy me!'

After he'd calmed down though, Darren found anxiety eating away at him. It could have been a press wind-up, it being not unknown for certain tabloid journalists to fake voices in order to get or confirm stories. But there was something about the voice, a certainty, a precision of tone, which suggested Sandor Whoever-He-Was knew something. Darren swallowed his pride and phoned Nick, unwittingly disturbing his bath night with the St Trinian's waitress that *he'd* ended up pulling after his misbegotten lunch with Kenny Dawes.

Despite the sploshing and giggling down the line, Darren had his worst fears confirmed. Kosics was kosher.

'He's the middle-man for most of the big Italian and Spanish clubs! He got all those Russians and

30

Romanians into the Italian League . . . Guys like him do a deal first then tell the player later!'

Nick pronounced this development so serious that he would come up first thing Monday to sort it. There was only one suspect – Derek Horsfield.

'Time to get heavy,' Nick had thought and his dress and demeanour reflected that. Sun-glasses, dark suit, attaché case in one hand, mobile phone in the other. The Agent From Hell look, designed to strike terror into the hearts of weak-chinned club chairmen through-out the land. He waltzed straight through the secre-tary's office and swung the door open on an apparently unperturbed Horsfield. Nick looked down on him through his dark lenses, waiting for a reaction.

'When you've finished playing Clint Eastwood, Nick, you can sit down!'

Nick put his phone and his case on Horsfield's desk.

'I. Am very angry. With you.'

Horsfield scoffed.

'Blimey, now it's Michael Caine!'

Nick sat down and removed his sun-glasses and fixed Horsfield with a humourless stare.

'I want to know why my client is being touted around Europe without either his or my permission,' he said firmly, adding 'ass-hole' for greater effect. It had none. Horsfield just smiled. Confident. Secure. In charge.

'Now don't be rude or I'll throw you out.'

Nick made one last stab at intimidation.

'Not before I hang you out of that window by your ankles!'

Horsfield chuckled to himself.

'Leave off, Nick. Everyone knows you're more Mill-field than Millwall! Now listen – straight up. I had no choice. The bank are threatening to send in the heavy

31

mob. Last week they fingered Darren as our best asset . . .'

'So you went behind his back and mine?' Nick asked, already knowing the answer. Horsfield shrugged.

'If we'd been able to agree terms last week, I'd have toughed it out with the bank.'

Nick snorted. 'You made us a derisory offer to provoke us into holding out. Selling an apparently disloyal player doesn't look half as bad as dumping a faithful servant!'

Horsfield brought his hands together in an unwitting gesture of prayer.

'Nick, I'm a fan. I love Darren! I panicked. I needed some help! That's why I brought Kosics in. And he delivered, even gave me my cash advance back! But, look – if we could agree a deal for Darren now, I'd tell the bank, Kosics *and* Sampdoria to take a long walk off a short pier!'

Nick smiled. He'd just seen a weak spot in Horsfield's defence. He tried to open it some more.

'Funnily enough, that's what Darren seems to want.'

Horsfield looked at him joyously and stood up.

'Let's do it then! I'll go to an extra grand a week. Even if it has to come out of my own pocket!'

The defence had gone. This was better than violence. Much better. Nick had him by the balls, now was the time to twist.

'Sorry, Derek, I represent Darren's *interests*, not his wishes. He'd be a guaranteed millionaire if Sampdoria buy him. I won't stand in the way of that. It'd be, well, *unprofessional*.' Nick smirked.

Horsfield felt his stomach turn over. He'd just gifted a two-million-pound-plus transfer to Nick Young. 'Gutted' couldn't do justice to the feeling.

'You bastard!'

'You shouldn't go in the deep-end if all you do is the doggy-paddle, Derek!'

Nick bought a bottle of champagne for himself in the first wine-bar he could find in the town. Non-vintage unfortunately, but it tasted as good as the top marque in the best year. It was all his deal now. If Sampdoria's interest was genuine, which it appeared to be, he could delay the transfer until Darren's contract formally expired. That meant his transfer fee would not be subject to negotiation but simply based on a wage-rate and years-of-service formula. It might creep up to £1 million – about half of what Horsfield had expected – and the rest would go to Darren in a boffo signing-on fee and three-year contract package. Kosics would get his commission and be told to fuck off out of it. It was beautiful. Only one detail remained: persuading Darren to accept the move.

The first indications were bad. For one thing, Darren brought Claire to the wine-bar with him, which put Nick on edge – she was too sarky by half. Too likely to pull Darren away from him. So Nick finessed it, telling Darren in funereal tones that Horsfield couldn't agree terms, and that the move to Sampdoria looked the only option.

Darren gave him an accusing look, but Nick brazened it out.

'I don't see why you should fret. You'll be made for life!'

'Crippled more like, the way they play over in Italy! I don't need *this*, Nick. Not now. The boss only needs the slightest excuse not to pick me again.'

Nick shrugged, feigning sympathy.

'Well, it looks like you're leaving anyway!'

So far so good. Then Claire, who looked as though she'd been running an imaginary lie-detector on Nick, intervened.

'Spoken like a true agent! Darren's flogged his guts out for this team and you expect him to pull up his roots just like that?'

Nick winced. 'I think I preferred it when he wouldn't talk business in front of you.'

A tense silence fell. Nick felt things slipping away. He could sense Darren chickening out. Opting for the quiet life.

'If we can leave sentiment aside, you're well out of this club, Darren. They'll always be selling to survive, not buying to succeed.'

Darren couldn't deny the point. His mind was in turmoil. He felt like he'd been picked up by a whirlwind and didn't know where on earth he'd be dumped by it. Then another thought occurred.

'What about the damage a move would do to any England career I might have?'

'If you succeed over there it will *enhance* your international prospects!' Nick answered slickly.

'But I'm a novice. Once I move abroad I'll be out of sight and out of mind! So bollocks to it!' Darren stood up and headed for the bar.

'God, he could be hard work,' Nick thought. Claire stared at him stonily. He gave her a plaintive gesture.

'Most players would get down on bended Armanis for the chance to play in Italy! You've lived abroad, haven't you? Tell him how good it can be!'

Claire said nothing, leaving Nick to fear that the deal would go down. If Darren settled for staying put on a peanuts wage-rate, Nick would be off. Agents could have no time for losers.

By the middle of the week, however, a sort of desultory momentum to the transfer had been generated. Sampdoria *were* interested enough to come over for a meeting in London. Horsfield had resigned himself to selling Darren and appeasing Ed the bank manager. Ray Peters had frozen Darren out, so Darren had thought he might as well listen to what the Genoese club had to say. It was only the tabloid press who made European transfers sound glamorous. They were often, as this one was, a misguided alliance between one club struggling for money and another seeking positive headlines in its own region, with a player at the heart of it who had no real idea what he was getting into, apart from a highly exaggerated pile of money.

Darren had tried to balance his disappointment at his own club's attitude to him after nearly ten years of service by working up an enthusiasm for life in Italy. He'd seen the Serie A games on Channel 4. They had a good technical quality, probably too good for him, but there were an awful lot of clubs unable to keep up with the big boys of Juventus, Inter and Milan. If you were outside these big three, it seemed to Darren, you were just competing to survive.

He flicked through his mental index file on British forwards who'd gone abroad; there were more debits than credits. Ian Rush, Luther Blissett, Mark Hateley, David Platt had all found goals, and a regular place in their teams, hard to achieve. Kevin Keegan and Tony Woodcock in Germany, and Gary Lineker in Spain – they'd pulled it off. So the odds on him succeeding in Italy seemed long. Better money and more sunshine didn't stack as high as the risk of professional failure and isolation from the national team.

So despite Nick Young's off-stage promptings, Darren settled on a restrained rather than an enthusiastic tone to the meeting at the Portman Hotel with two smartly blazered officials from Sampdoria. They were accompanied by Kosics, while Darren was flanked by Nick and Horsfield. As coffee was poured the senior Sampdoria official broke the ice.

'Signor Kosics showed us a very impressive video of your goal-scoring, Darren.'

Darren nodded dutifully, wondering how in hell they'd got that together and what it might contain. His five goals against Swanside Comprehensive in 1975?

'I hope you'll have to bring one out for the goals I score with Sampdoria . . .'

The official smiled at this show of confidence.

'Bravo! We all liked the moment when you scored the hat-trick. You went not to the team, but to the fans! In Italy, this would make you very popular!'

'If I get a hat-trick in Italy I could run for Pope, couldn't I?'

Darren felt Nick's shoe kick his shin under the coffee table. The Italians smiled, but were plainly not amused. It probably prompted their next, pointed, question.

'A smattering of English . . .'

More polite laughter. Was this a good sign? Was he coming across as witty or as a tedious dick-head with a sub-Gazza complex? Darren just didn't know, he'd never had to audition before. His head swam. Now he heard himself asking the Italians a question!

'I wonder if you could tell me what the situation would be with your other foreign players? Would I be, well, guaranteed a first-team place?'

Nick Young hid his forehead in his hands.

'Nobody can have such a guarantee,' said the main official, with a distinct frostiness in his voice.

Darren realised he'd goofed and trod water.

'What I meant was . . . well . . . I wouldn't want to be just rotated among them.'

'As I said, there are no guarantees. But we do not spend big money foolishly.' That was about as reassuring as the Italians could get. An awkward silence fell. Kosics leant forward.

'Can we just confirm the expiry date of your current contract?'

'June,' said Nick quickly.

'Of next year,' added Horsfield, who was still hoping that particular loophole could be closed. He could see the deal ebbing away at this rate. Darren was coming across as a bolshie little git. He checked his watch and lifted Darren up by his elbow.

'Gentlemen, may I ask that you excuse Darren now. He must join up with the team for tonight's very important game. The manager has already given special dispensation for this meeting!'

'Like hell he has!' thought Darren as he came to his feet. There was another round of handshakes.

'Very nice to meet you all!' Darren said lamely, hoping to recover some lost ground.

Nick escorted him towards the exit. He hissed into Darren's ear. 'Did your best to blow it there, didn't you? *You* don't make demands! And I told you not to mention the Pope!'

'Sorry. It just came out. Besides it's better for them to see who they might be buying . . . an ordinary lad, not some bloody international diplomat!'

'I'll tell them you were very nervous, that'll do it.'

'You can tell them I was very unimpressed.'

Nick shoved his face right into Darren's. 'We've got 'em all by the balls here! Horsfield's been bullshitting them about your current contract. If I delay the deal till you're *out*-of-contract, Sampdoria would only have to pay ten times your current wage as the fee! Then I get you a big slice of what they're saving!'

Far from being elated at the thought, Darren looked thoroughly disheartened.

'I never knew there was this much integrity in transfer deals.'

'Right, off you go – and for Christ's sake don't do a

Gazza and get injured the night before the deal of your life!'

Darren tugged his forelock in response. He pushed through the revolving door and headed for the cab rank. He couldn't now remember a single detail of the meeting, apart from a vague feeling that some perverse instinct of his own had put the whole deal in jeopardy.

Nick watched him go, angry but relieved. Some smart talking was needed now. He took a deep breath, straightened the lines of his suit and headed across the lobby towards the toilet. As he went in, a dark-haired middle-aged man in a lightweight suit rose from one of the sofas in the lobby and followed him in.

Nick splashed his face with water, dried it with a towel, polished his glasses and turned back to the door. The man from the lobby stepped in front of him. For a split second Nick had a sudden dread.

'Mr Young?'

Nick's mind raced – the Tax, the VAT?

'Yeah, what?'

The man took out a business card bearing a crest and thrust it at a stunned Nick.

'Please don't sign anything until you have talked to us first. I am in Room 307.'

After the previous Saturday's debacle, Darren had been restored to the team by Ray Peters. It was almost certainly a reluctant gesture, but the game this evening was against the League leaders, Kenny Dawes's team. A victory would close the gap, keeping the title race wide open for the last few weeks. The burden on Darren was enormous, he'd taken stick from the crowd and on the local radio phone-in for letting the team down. He knew he owed the fans a performance tonight, and as he sat in the dressing-room, smearing Vaseline on his eyebrows to staunch the flow of sweat

38

during the game, he tried desperately to clear his mind
of all that had gone on in the past ten days. England,
transfers, big money, Jane, moving house, Claire, rows
with Nick, crapped-on by the chairman – forget it!
Forget it all, son!

In the visitors' dressing-room preparations were no
less intense. Dawes knew what to expect and he wasn't
about to let a season's work go down the drain. His
team was battle-hardened, immune to the critics who
sniped at their long-ball, all-action game, but one last
exhortation wouldn't go amiss. Dawes took the centre
of the floor and pointed through the door to where the
home dressing-room was situated. As he began to pace,
he looked each of his players in the eye for signs of
weakness or nerves.

'This team . . . is in our way. They can stop us getting
what we want. But *we* – are not going to let them do
that. We are gonna run the bollocks off them! We are
gonna hit them hard. We are gonna destroy them! No
space, no time to think, no time to move, nowhere to
hide. They get nothing. Understand? *Nothing!*'

The players let out a spontaneous yell, like para-
troopers preparing for a drop. Dawes now stood over
his giant centre-half and put his hands on his shoulders.
He lowered his head menacingly. This was private
advice.

'First chance you get, give Matthews a whack. Hard,
right? Then verbal him. Shit on him. Do it till his head
goes. He's all they've got. Break him, and we've got
'em beaten!'

The centre-half nodded and flexed his shoulders like
a boxer pumped up by his corner-man. Tonight would
be a battle.

Up in the more civilised arena of the directors' box,
Horsfield was greeting all and sundry with a smile. This
was less to do with an expectation of victory than the

long and apparently fruitful lunch he'd enjoyed with the Sampdoria officials. The transfer looked on. Nick Young pushed through and installed himself in the next seat.

'Any of the Sampdoria mob come up?' Nick asked innocently.

'Nah, they're gonna watch this on satellite. If Darren has a good game, we've clinched it. I'm sure.'

'Me too,' Nick said with a private smile. He turned to survey the worthies in the box. All the usual faces, plus some once-a-year visitors because of the match's importance. But best of all, three rows back, was the guy who'd approached him in the hotel toilets. Nick gave him a discreet little wave. Then there was a huge roar of anticipation from the crowd as the two teams ran out, and all eyes were on the players.

The match began at a furious pace. It was clear that Darren's team were not going to sit back and slowly construct a strategy for victory, they were simply going to get the ball forward as much as possible and see if Darren could work his magic.

But the second time he got the ball he was taken down violently from behind by the centre-half. Darren tumbled to the turf, clutching his ankle and writhing in pain. In the stands Freddie Matthews and Claire, sitting together, winced and watched anxiously. This was the worst part of watching a loved-one play – missing a goal was neither here nor there, but serious injury was the worst nightmare.

Slowly, Darren recovered, aided by the freezing spray of the physio which numbed the area just above the boot and below the protective padding which the defender had expertly targeted. There would be a welter of bruising there in the morning, but for the next eighty-eight minutes he wouldn't allow himself to feel any pain. He worked the ankle a couple of times, and a cheer went up from the crowd. In the directors' box, Horsfield leant into Nick Young's ear.

'I keep seeing this hand holding a lighted match to a pile of bank-notes.'

Nick laughed. He could afford to, he knew how much bigger Darren's pile would be, and what currency it would be in.

Dawes's team weathered the first fifteen minutes of outright attacking by the home side and even began to build the odd breakaway for themselves. After one, they won a corner-kick. Darren spotted his marker going up to add his height and followed him back. At six feet one, and with a good standing jump in his armoury, Darren was often called back to defend such set-pieces. This time, however, it all went horribly wrong.

The kick was swung in very fast to the near-post. Instinctively, every player moved towards the ball's flight. But a flick from their centre-forward now looped the ball towards the back-post. Darren had lost sight of the ball. He felt the centre-half brush past him in a blur of arms and legs. Darren threw himself desperately at the ball, but the centre-half had beaten him. He powered a header down and into the net. One–nil to Dawes's team.

The visiting supporters danced and cheered, while all eyes in the defence searched for someone to blame. In this instant post-mortem, Darren looked the obvious suspect. He knew it himself. The corner should have been cleared at the near-post first, but then he should have been more alert. He hung his head. The team captain, Steve Hampson, raged at him for the cardinal sin – ball-watching. Darren trotted back upfield for the restart, feeling a stone heavier with the pressure.

Dawes's team sat back now, filling midfield, denying space, content with their lead. For the next hour,

Darren could achieve nothing. He faked runs, he twisted, he turned, he went wide, he went down the middle, but always there were two defenders to deny him the ball.

With less than ten minutes left, he finally broke free of his marker, faking a run into the box, then stopping and turning back to receive a ball to his feet. He had a split second to turn and face the goal and saw the wrong-footed defender scrambling back towards him. He waited for the lunge and nudged the ball to the right and past the sprawling tackle. There was no time to look up. He transferred a shaft of energy from brain to foot and, keeping his head down, slammed the ball with all his power. He knew he'd caught it as sweetly as possible. There was no jar, virtually no sense of impact, just a sensation of flowing power. He looked up to see the ball fly high past the goalkeeper's dive and smash into the stanchion at the back of the net: 1–1!

Electrified, Darren ran, not to the crowd, but to collect the ball. This was no time for self-indulgence. Every second counted. The home crowd celebrated and roared, their dream was still alive.

Dawes's team reeled, hanging on for the final whistle as the noise and the attacks blended into an overwhelming cacophony. Nick and Horsfield twitched and checked watches, while Freddie and Claire shouted Darren on.

With a minute to go, the ball was worked wide to Stevie Thomas the winger. He took on the left-back and sprinted to the by-line. In one movement he crossed. As the ball curled in and Darren moved towards it, he was taken in the chest by the centre-half's shoulder. Darren knew it was deliberate. More importantly, so did the referee. Penalty!

As he recovered his breath, Darren checked the eyes

42

of his team-mates. He was the usual penalty taker and nobody else was bidding for the job. Darren spotted the ball and took a brief look at the keeper flexing his legs and spreading his arms in intimidation. Darren backed away. He could virtually hear his dad's voice: 'Low, son, hit it low. Go for a five!' Darren turned and ran in at pace and curled the ball with precision towards the bottom right-hand corner. But the keeper had chanced his luck, dived that way a second before the ball had been struck. He pawed the ball down with his outstretched left hand and curled up joyously on the ball.

Darren slumped to the turf, his face covered by his hands. The hopes of the fans and his team-mates seemed to pass right through his gut like a dying flame. Within seconds the referee had blown the final whistle and Dawes and his players were celebrating the draw which preserved their lead and killed off this particular challenge.

In the home dressing-room there was a cavernous silence which was broken only by a vituperative outburst by the captain Hampson.

'If somebody hadn't been busy negotiating his way out of here we'd have had five more points out of these last two games!'

It was aimed at Darren, but Ray Peters was in quick to stop the recriminations spreading.

'That's enough. Nobody gets slaughtered for tonight!'

Hampson tossed his shirt across the room and headed for the plunge-bath. He jabbed a finger at Darren.

'He knows! He bloody knows!'

Darren didn't need the prosecution. He'd already found himself guilty. As he stood in a quiet corner of the players' lounge later, backed up against photos of the club's many teams, he felt like he never wanted to play football again. Nick Young approached. Darren dodged his look.

'Come on – head up. It happens to the best.'

'Yeah, but I'm not one of them.'

Nick smiled. 'You couldn't be more wrong. You are a very sought-after young man!'

'I must have blown it with the Italians,' Darren said bleakly.

'Maybe, maybe not – but there's been another bid.'

Darren looked up. Nick paused as Kenny Dawes bustled past, pausing to pat Darren on the shoulder.

'Unlucky, son. You tore us apart tonight. Don't let him get down, Nick!' Dawes winked and moved away. Darren saw the moment and guessed.

'Not *him*?'

Nick laughed. 'No! Kenny doesn't even rate you actually!'

Darren followed Dawes's triumphal progress through the room.

'I wish I'd known before I took the penalty – I'd have buried it . . .'

Nick tried to smooth over his tactless gaff.

'Anyway, who cares?' he said, leaning across and tapping the photos behind Darren. 'You're history here, now! "There is some corner of a foreign field . . ."'

Darren eye-balled him with exasperation.

'Who the *hell* is it?'

Once Kosics had alerted the major clubs to Darren's availability, it had become not a question of calmly exploring the various offers, but of managing a short-lived feeding frenzy. Such was the in-fighting on the European soccer circuit that transfers were as much a part of the ego wars as any competitive football match. If rumours of one club making a move circulated, others

44

would be provoked. F.C. Barcelona, the Spanish League champions, and one of the richest clubs in Europe, had no intention of losing out to Sampdoria. They'd beaten them in the European Cup Final at Wembley in 1992, and that psychological ascendancy had to be maintained. Vice-President Roberto Gamez, had been instructed to shadow Sampdoria's negotiations and to make sure that Darren became a Barcelona player.

Darren couldn't begin to articulate his reactions to Nick's news. He was mentally numbed by the night's defeat and the sense of rupture with the club he had loved since childhood. His ankle began to throb as he lay flat on his back in bed, watched carefully by Claire. The move seemed just as unreal as anything else in his head. It took Claire's reaction to jolt him into life.

'Barcelona? Barca-bloody-lona! That's fantastic, isn't it?' she exclaimed.

'Well, yeah – you're not kidding. I mean, if I think about it I start shaking . . .'

'Nick asked me to have a word with you the other day. Persuade you that living abroad could work.'

'Why didn't you?'

'It's your life. Should be your decision,' Claire said, turning away so she couldn't see Darren's reaction.

'Well, it's like this – I thought I'd come a long way already. You know, compared to my dad. But then I suppose, here I am, still in my home town, still with the one club . . .'

Claire turned back to him: '. . . with a suburban house and a money-grabbing girlfriend?'

Darren smiled at her.

'Look – I, er, if it happens, I want you to come with me. I don't think I could manage without you . . .'

'Thought they wanted you as a player.'

Darren looked at her lovingly. He would need her

45

wit and her common sense to survive out there in Spain.
'I'll take that as a "no", shall I?' he teased.

Claire dived under the duvet.

'Mind my ankle!' roared Darren.

Within ten days the deal was done. £1.5 million was
the agreed fee, which Darren thought was a fair legacy
to his club. They might even name a stand after him.
The rest of the players didn't seem to resent him. He
was given a sombrero and some pink lip-salve at the
last training session – 'You get kissed a lot over there,'
Steve Thomas chortled. The only dampener came from
the England manager – he thought Darren should drop
out of the squad while the transfer was in progress.
Pretty much as Darren had feared. But if he succeeded
in Spain . . .

Darren took a last look at the ground with his dad.
The bulldozers were due in that week to knock down
the terracing where they'd always stood. The game was
changing in so many ways now. Big business involvement, more comfort, satellite TV – nobody could tell
whether it would all work or be a footballing version
of the 'South Sea Bubble'. It was probably a good time
to be abroad.

Freddie teased Darren about missing the local beer.
Darren retaliated. 'Now you've got a new song to
learn . . .'

Freddie looked curious. Darren whistled the tune to
'Guantanamera' and launched into verse . . .

> 'Hay uno Darren Matthews . . .
> Solo uno Darren Matthews!'

Chapter Three

Claire and Darren actually made it out of the flat on time. There'd been only two rows throughout the whole week-long process of packing, each about what Claire should wear for the trip and what her clothes might say to the Spanish media waiting at Barcelona Airport. Darren had been too harassed to think about such things until Claire had pointed out that the impression made by her would probably reflect very much on him.

Was she, for example, his prim-and-proper English rose girlfriend? Or his hip, fashion-designer companion? Or did Darren want her to be seen as a beach bimbo with the attention span of a Club Med holiday? This last was, of course, Claire being ironic, but it helped get the point across to Darren. Sportingly, he'd suggested that Claire should wear some of her own designs . . . 'Might take some of the attention off the pasty-faced prat alongside you.'

Claire had duly provided the compliment which this remark was supposed to generate, realising with surprise that Darren was actually shredded by nervousness. He was on the brink of a complete life change. There was no turning back now. Sink-or-swim time, or, as he put it at one point, 'Like going sky-diving without knowing if the parachutes would open.'

He'd briefly attempted to cajole her into a last bout of passion before they left the apartment, but their tight

47

schedule had prevented it. Now as they lugged their cases across the communal grounds in the silence of an English mid-summer dawn, exactly as thousands of package holidaymakers throughout Britain would be doing, the banality of this start to a new life struck Darren. Where were the stretch-limos, the marching-bands, the farewell crowds?

But at least one supporter had seen fit to give Darren a farewell message. As they reached his BMW saloon, he spotted the two flat-tyres at the front and quickly confirmed that they had two companions at the back. A quadruple puncture was long odds, and the livid red aerosol spray across the windscreen and down the car's sides confirmed a vengeful act of vandalism. 'Judas' was the simple graffito, a last comment by a disgruntled fan on Darren leaving the club.

'Why couldn't they let me leave the country in peace?' he asked fruitlessly.

'The only surprise is that they could spell Judas,' added Claire as they stared at the immobilised car. Darren ran back to the flat to phone for a taxi, and soon they were on their way to the airport.

They made up some of the time, and arrived without further incidents, but once inside the terminal there was another unpleasant surprise waiting for them. Nick Young was expected – he would be sorting out Darren's finances and having a last look at the contract before signature – but his two companions at the gate had a suspiciously journalistic look about them.

A tall, thin, stubbled youth, dressed all in black, stood over a camera-bag, with a top-of-the-range Nikon slung around his neck. Darren paused for a moment trying to work out what was going on. Claire offered an explanation. 'This may be my fault. The *News of the World* phoned yesterday asking if they could take some shots of us leaving. I forgot to mention it.'

But this didn't account for the modishly dressed thirty-something woman in Ray-Bans who also seemed to be a travelling companion. Darren considered several possibilities, the least unlikely of which was that Nick had simply picked her up either that very morning or the night before. Despite his owlish, almost bookish appearance, Nick had a peculiar ability to generate sexual encounters at the slightest opportunity. He certainly looked pleased with himself as he greeted Darren and Claire. Then the truth was revealed.

'Darren, this is Lindy Barge of *Hello* magazine, and Jasper her photographer . . . !'

Darren exchanged a look of forboding with Claire, which Lindy plainly picked up on. Her cursory 'Hi' went well below the affected ennui of the practised style-journalist. Nick soldiered on unwittingly.

'And this is Darren's . . . well, fiancée, I suppose! Claire Travis!'

Claire and Lindy exchanged the merest of handshakes, with Claire aware that her clothes were being checked out for instantaneous judgement.

'How quaint. I didn't think people got engaged any more!' Lindy said with a smile.

Nick could at least now sense that a sticky start had been achieved. He stepped in to try and repair some of the damage.

'Lindy and Jasper are coming over to Barcelona with us for a couple of days to do a little feature about how you settle in!'

Darren looked like he was about to turn on his heels and go back home.

'Can I have a word, Nick?'

Darren moved towards one of the windows overlooking the aircraft bay. The Iberia jet was being loaded with supplies, the most vital for Darren at that precise moment being the sick-bags. Nick tried to get in first.

'Before you start moaning, they're paying ten grand for this. That'll buy a lot of bathroom tiles for the new hacienda!'

'Why *Hello*? The only member of the Royal Family I know is *Joe* Royle at Oldham Athletic . . . I'm just a footballer!'

'You *were*! Now you're a Euro-celebrity! Footballers have got a different status on the Continent. They rub shoulder-pads with the stars!'

'I'm more shin-pads, in case you hadn't noticed!'

'Look,' Nick pleaded, 'they're gonna run this in their Spanish edition too – it's called *Hola*.'

'Yes, I'm with you . . .' Darren replied acidly.

'So we score a *double*-whammy! The English get a glimpse of your sophisticated new life-style, while the Spanish see that you're *not* some tattooed berk with his bum hanging out of a pair of Union Jack shorts! It's got to be better than a double-page spread in the *Daily Sport*!'

Darren watched the final pod of ready-cooked meals being inserted into the plane's hold. He felt as processed as they must be. But there was no time to correct the packaging of himself while the transfer itself was in progress. His chance would only come when all this preliminary bollocks was over and he got down to meeting his new team-mates on a training pitch. For now, it was simply a case of grinning and bearing it until *Hello* had said 'Goodbye'.

Across the lounge, Lindy watched Nick and Darren in animated conversation.

'Is Darren always so . . . sensitive about the press?' Lindy probed.

Claire gave her a sweet smile. 'It might be because we thought you were from the tabloids . . .' Claire watched the insult hit home.

'Did you hear that, Jasper? Miss Travis here thought we looked more grubby than glossy.'

Jasper chewed gum disinterestedly. Lindy pointed into the corridor outside.

'Now this chap looks more of a *News of the World* type to me!"

Claire turned. A perspiring, circumferentially challenged man, with two cameras hanging from his neck, waddled into the lounge waving cheerily. Under his arm he carried two straw sombreros and a large, fluffy toy donkey.

'Just a quick snap of you leaving, for the diary page, Darren!' he panted, handing out the essential 'Spanish' props for the photograph. Darren suffered in silence both throughout this little 'tabloid' session and again during the flight. Any moment of intimacy – holding Claire's hand, browsing through a phrase-book, taking a first look down on the spectacular red-roofed sprawl of Barcelona – became a photo-opportunity for Jasper. But this intrusion became a minor irritation compared to the reception awaiting Darren at the city's smoked-glass and marble airport terminal.

Roberto Gamez, the FC Barcelona Vice-President who had orchestrated the transfer came on board the plane to greet Darren, and then led him, with Claire and Nick following, out through the VIP lounge. So much for Claire's wardrobe tantrum – she was barely noticed by the three dozen or so photographers who filled the corridor before them, backed up by five television camera-crews with their lights blazing, and perhaps a dozen more radio journalists trying desperately to snatch a word with Darren, or at least give a first impression of the club's latest signing.

Gamez beamed throughout the battle down through the Arrivals lounge and out onto the terminal road. It was plainly meant to be his 'show', with Darren as star guest.

The bulging crowd moved as though it was physically attached to them. Darren glimpsed red and blue flags being waved by Barcelona supporters, and now somewhere in the melee a trumpet sounded a charge and a chant of 'Barca! Barca! Barca!' went echoing round the steel girders and Egyptian palm-trees which framed the hall. With a protective cordon of armed Guardia Civil officers now at hand, Darren found himself bundled out of the air-conditioned unreality of the terminal and into the glorious, instant heat of a Barcelona mid-day.

Before he could savour the soft, warm air, strong hands pushed him into the back seat of a large Mercedes limousine, where he was joined by a shell-shocked Claire and a harassed Nick. Gamez climbed in after a last wave to the photographers, and almost before the door had closed, the limo pulled away, flanked by two police out-riders on motor-bikes, complete with flashing lights and sirens. Only five hours ago, Darren had been looking at four punctures and phoning a mini-cab . . .

The journey into Barcelona was largely a chance for Darren and Claire to spot various landmarks familiar from the television coverage of the 1992 Olympics: to their right was the Olympic Stadium with the futuristic appendage which looked like a record stylus. Up on the range of hills which looked down on the city was the lager-can shape of the Norman Foster designed communications tower.

As the limo sped on down the main route into the city, Claire leant forward to see if she could catch a glimpse of the 'asparagus spires' of the 'Sagrada Familia' cathedral, 'that bizarre monument to architect Antonio Gaudi's tripped-out visions', as one of the backpackers' guides had described it.

Darren, who hadn't heard of it at all, wondered how Claire had managed to find the time to read up on the city. He was quietly triumphant then to hear Gamez tell Claire that the still incomplete cathedral was much further over in the city. Her attempt at showing Gamez how cultured she was had backfired. She was like one of those American tourists in London who expect to find the Tower of London backing on to Buckingham Palace.

The car had now pulled off the main route, and was travelling quickly through a canyon of modish apartment blocks, draped with hanging vines and window-boxes. The skyline suddenly cleared and the profile of Barcelona's huge Nou Camp Stadium appeared. Darren thought it was a bit like having a football ground in Knightsbridge.

'Here is our own little cathedral,' Gamez said with a knowing smile, watching Darren go quiet as the sheer size of the club's sporting complex imposed itself upon him. The limo turned in through guarded gates and sped across an expanse of car-park to a marble-and-glass entrance hall where a further press and TV entourage was now encamped.

Darren was again separated from Claire and Nick as Gamez led him in and then invited him to climb a wide staircase. All around him were paintings, sculptures, mosaics depicting football action, making the club look more like an art gallery than a ground. Now they were turning off into a corridor and Darren caught sight of the club's own museum, a huge, brightly lit exhibition area, lined with glittering silver trophies.

He was dizzied by this sudden propulsion into the sophisticated and historic set-up of the Barcelona club. He'd picked up a bit about its history from various sources, and knew that it was regarded as a bit special by all who'd played there. He'd even read in one book about the club's symbolic importance to the people of Catalonia, who'd suffered greatly for their independent spirit in the darker days of the dictator General Franco's regime.

After the Civil War, the football ground had become one of the few places where they could speak Catalan, their own language, which Franco tried to eradicate. Darren had once tried to explain this to his dad in terms of Geordie or Scouse being banned by London, and confined to the terraces of St James's Park or Anfield, but the point of the information had lost its impact on Freddie who thought this would be quite a good move for Darren.

None of the reading and the phone-calls, though, had prepared Darren for the sheer majesty of the Nou Camp set-up. Everything about it said 'first class', and that included the medical room into which he was now escorted for a pre-signing check-up ceremony. He hoped the club's doctors would understand that his rapid heartbeat was present not out of illness, but out of sheer excitement at his new surroundings.

While Darren was put through his medical, Claire and Nick were taken by Gamez to a sumptuous committee room to meet the club's President, Jose-Luis Vaqueras, a tall, elegantly dressed man in his early fifties, with a calm but authoritative manner. Nick guessed that a slight bow of the head wouldn't go amiss with the opening handshake.

'How nice to put a face to all the faxes!' Nick said, enunciating carefully for Vaqueras's benefit. The President gave a wink and replied in English a shade better than Nick's.

'Your boy had better be worth all this money we're paying, Mr Young.'

Nick nodded as graciously as he could, sensing

instantly that Vaqueras was not a guy to be either patronised in conversation or under-estimated in deals. Nick went straight into full diplomatic mode.

'Darren is very keen to fulfil all the expectations of such a great club as F.C. Barcelona!'

Vaqueras gave him a smile of approval, before approaching Claire.

'And who is this elegant young lady? Your wife, Mr Young?'

Gamez intervened deferentially, leaving no doubt as to the gulf in status between vice-president and president.

'No, this is Senorita Claire Travis, Matthews's girl-friend, Senor Vaqueras.'

Vaqueras swooped for Claire's hand and kissed it. She plucked out a phrase she'd remembered from her Berlitz reading. *'Mucho gusto, Senor Presidente!'* hoping that it meant something like 'pleased to meet you'. It obviously did because Vaqueras exclaimed with delight, 'Bravo, my dear! I am delighted to make your acquaintance! You will enjoy your time here in Barcelona!'

They all smiled at each other, so far so good. For Darren, though, the niceties had given way to a punishing series of medical tests while he jogged on a motorised running-machine. With his chest wired up to a cardiograph, and his mouth wrapped round a breathing tube, Darren felt as though he was auditioning for NASA's space programme rather than pitching for two games of football a week.

His eyes were tested, his groin and abdomen checked for hernias, the alignment of his legs was examined for bone damage and even when he was finally allowed to flop onto a towel-covered examination couch, the doctor pounced to take his blood pressure. Darren recovered his breath, waiting for the stone-faced doctor to give some indication of approval – a rubber-stamp on his bum, maybe?

Finally the Doctor smiled as he unwrapped the rubber sleeve from Darren's left arm.

'Everything is fine, Darren. You are in top-class condition.'

'Thank God for that. I haven't trained for over three weeks!'

The doctor took a small syringe from a tray behind him.

'Now we just need a small sample of your blood . . .'

'I'm Group O . . .' Darren said, hoping to pre-empt the needle.

'Thank you . . . but this is for an HIV test.'

Darren looked at the doctor, offended by the request.

'AIDS? Well, you've no worries on that score! My fiancée's upstairs – she'll vouch for me!'

'AIDS is still a threat to people of heterosexual lifestyle, you know?' The doctor looked at him sternly. Darren wondered if one of the machines he'd been wired up to might have been a lie-detector.

'Well, yeah, but I'm careful. Always have been,' he said defensively. It didn't satisfy the doctor.

'And have you had many partners?'

'Christ,' thought Darren, 'what do they want here, names and addresses? What's the Spanish average for conquests, ten or twenty fewer than the average randy Brit?' Before he could think further, he found himself on the verge of referring to 'the Spanish Inquis . . .', but stopped himself just short of out-right offence. He lay back and let the doctor take the blood sample he required. He *had* been 'careful' most of the time, he reassured himself. Hadn't he?

Ten minutes later, Darren was back in his suit and being marched into a committee room, flanked by

Gamez and Vaqueras. A table had been set up for dozens of radio microphones, and the TV lights lifted the temperature into the high 80s, despite the air-conditioning. The medical would seem a breeze compared to this, his first press conference, and Gamez was quickly into an announcement through the microphones, as they took their seats behind the table, with Nick Young sliding in at the end in case Darren needed help.

'*Senores – el delantero Ingles!* Darren Matthews!'

Darren got the gist of that easily enough – he knew already that '*delantero*' was the Spanish name for a forward, but also that he would be struggling for vocabulary beyond that and 'hello', 'good-bye', and 'thank you'. So he made do with smiles and a little wave, and then the pen was thrust into his hand for him to confirm his pact with F.C. Barcelona. Darren signed the contract carefully and then it was done; nothing could stop him now! He belonged to a famous institution.

The flashes of the photographers' cameras strobed the room as Darren and President Vaqueras shook hands. Now it was time for questions, with Gamez translating into Darren's ear.

It was pretty solemn stuff. He had to outline his hopes for his career with the club, and acknowledge the place of Barcelona in the spectrum of Catalonian patriotism. No, 'How did you feel when the ball hit the net stuff?' here!

Darren coped well, confessing his lack of Spanish, but vowing to learn, and sounding sincere when he talked of how impressed he'd been by the club and its links with Catalonian history. He was somewhat dismayed then to see a vaguely familiar English sports-desk face push forward to ask a question.

'Terry Corden, *Daily Mail*, London . . .' the face announced.

Darren smiled knowingly. He'd asked Nick to play down all the 'Englishman abroad' stuff that the papers back home had been trying to weedle out of him. For Darren to leave the country shouting the odds on his own success would have invited tabloid scepticism and intrigue. The quiet departure had worked up till now.

'How did you wangle the exes for this trip, Terry? You doing a travel piece as well?' Darren asked, hoping to deflect Corden from his purpose.

'I happened to be out here on a family holiday when the desk phoned, Darren! Now, can I ask you how you think you'll have to adapt to the Barcelona style?'

Darren tried to work out where the trip-wires were in the question and tiptoed ahead slowly.

'Well, I expect to see a lot more of the ball on the ground, slower build-ups, having to think more about what I do.'

It was too bland. Corden came back at him again.

'Are you intimidated by the prospect of tough, not to say, brutal man-to-man marking in the Spanish League?'

Here we go, thought Darren – the stitch-up. Anything I say now will be taken down, twisted, and turned into a 'cocky bastard slags off Spanish hit-men' headline for the delight of readers in Little England. Darren bought himself some time with a sip from a glass of water.

'I think that's a bit of a stereotype actually. Whatever country you play in, defenders want to stop forwards. I've been kicked from Sheffield to Southampton, so I'm not going to start worrying now.'

Darren hoped that would smother any fires Corden was trying to stoke. A Spanish journalist now pitched him a question, and while he waited for the translation, he caught a brief sighting of Claire standing on the edge of the room. She mimed applause in his direction and he gave her a grateful smile, feeling instantly less lonely.

The question – about who Darren hoped the new coach would be, the old one having just left – was an easy deflection round the post. It was nothing to do with him.

'Perhaps President Vaqueras knows?' Darren asked playfully. Vaqueras just smiled and put a finger to his lips.

For another half-hour or so, Darren fielded questions and gave sound-bites to local radio and television, before Vaqueras called a halt. Darren stretched himself and then slipped out of the room on the pretext of a pee, in reality seeking a quiet moment of his own to gather his thoughts.

He also wanted to get a precise sight of his new place of work. The mahogany-clad committee rooms and trophy cabinets were all very impressive, but they wouldn't figure much in his life once training got under way. His 'beat' was the underground dressing-room and the pitch itself.

Guessing at various doors along a corridor, Darren suddenly found himself stepping out into a great swathe of blue and red seating which stretched right around the cavernous concrete bowl in front of him. And row upon row of them reached up on several tiers above his head and way across the other side of the stadium too, until he had to virtually bend double to see the sky. Over 110,000 fans would be in place here for the really big games, about thirty thousand more than Wembley could now hold. Down on the lush green pitch, sprinklers were at work preparing the grass for the new league season. There was virtual silence. Darren tried to imagine the noise and the tumult cascading down upon him during a match and how he would cope with such pressure.

'There you are . . .' It was Claire. Darren turned and gestured to his new theatre.

'Look at it, Claire! It's fantastic! Can you imagine what it must be like to play here when it's full!'

'Quite a challenge,' she said quietly, giving his hand a squeeze of reassurance. 'Come on,' she beckoned, 'we've been invited for lunch by President Vaqueras.'

If Darren thought he'd got over the main obstacles of his first day in Barcelona he was soon to discover otherwise. First of all, it emerged at the traditionally styled Catalan restaurant, tucked away in a smart suburb of the city, that there was more to President Vaqueras than being the top man at Barcelona football club.

He had been born outside the region, but in his early twenties had inherited an old vineyard just outside Vilafranca in the Penedes area of Catalonia. Since then, he'd expanded and built up the business to become one of the major growers, and this success had helped his integration into Barcelona society. Like many 'immigrants', he had found in his new home a deep well of patriotism and identity which had enabled him to be elected to F.C. Barcelona's managing committee, and subsequently to the Presidency.

His stewardship of the club had been exemplary, with only a hint of conservatism to irritate the more active committee members such as Gamez. But here, around the lunch table, fuelled by the optimism which a new signing generated, they were colleagues in harmony. Darren certainly scented a cosy conspiracy as Vaqueras and Gamez put their heads together in earnest discussion. This was not about football, but two of the other Catalan obsessions, wine and food.

Soon bottles of Vaqueras's own wine were being opened at the table by a fawning sommelier, and after much sniffing and swirling, Vaqueras ordered glasses to be poured for Claire, Nick and Darren. Another lengthy conversation with the head waiter was summarised by Gamez for the benefit of the Brits.

'Senor Vaqueras is ordering several Catalan dishes for you to try – cold salad of cod with peppers and olives, cheeks of hake with garlic, partridge baked in vinegar, baby octopus . . .'

Darren gave a wan smile. 'I'm glad the medical wasn't this afternoon!'

The joke was lost on Vaqueras, for whom lunch was plainly a serious business. More than that, Darren felt he was being tested, perhaps even teased in some way, by being thrown straight into the deep end of Catalan gastronomy. He'd travelled abroad often, of course – holidays in the main since his old club had never managed to qualify for Europe. But his experience of foreign food was limited to what were now Anglicised clichés – lasagne, paella, that sort of thing. There was nothing for it now but to accept Vaqueras's hospitality in full.

And so, in true Barcelona style, the lunch became a three-and-a-half-hour assault course as dish after dish appeared at the table in no apparent order of seniority. Most of the creations were delicious, Darren thought, although the tide of oil and garlic became a little wearisome.

Claire was able to get away with accepting small portions by playing the 'must be careful of my diet' card, while Nick simply puffed out his cheeks and patted his stomach to dodge a round. It was therefore left to Darren to carry the burden of the meal, especially when the platter of tiny, pink octopuses was offered round.

By five o'clock they'd just finished a bottle of 'Cava', the local sparkling wine, and were moving onto liqueurs and cigars. Darren declined both, but still had to sit through Gamez, Vaqueras and Nick each smoking a huge Havana cigar. At times the fug obscured the table, with the three glowing torpedoes of tobacco looking like the stacks of a 1950s power-station.

Eventually, at six, they were free. Kisses and handshakes were exchanged, the food test had been passed. Darren, Nick and Claire had their limo take them straight to the hotel which the club had booked for them.

Darren was exhausted by now, and probably three-parts drunk as well. The tedious formalities in the hotel of registering became confusing, especially when the hotel insisted that the bills would not be settled by the club. Darren had ditched his UK credit cards, brought little cash and no travellers' cheques on the quite reasonable assumption, in the circumstances, that he'd have all this provided by his new employers. It fell to Claire therefore to guarantee their stay with her credit card, and to cash some of her travellers' cheques for spending money.

Nick was little help, too busy trying to work out who the Mr Brown who'd left two messages at the hotel might be.

'Probably the guy doing your new boot deal,' he guessed to a completely indifferent Darren, who wanted slippers now, and pyjamas, and a cup of tea after a long bath and then a quiet night between cool cotton sheets.

That he enjoyed none of these things was due to nothing less than his own imprudence. He should have approached the lunch more cautiously, rather than affecting a gung-ho appetite for Vaqueras's gastronomic tour. This was now what his throbbing head was telling him. He'd got two wheels down fine – the medical, the press conference – but now the under-carriage on the third was playing up. Darren plunged into the bathroom and held on for dear life.

*   *   *

A simple fruit and croissant breakfast on the hotel's sunny terrace the next morning represented the first sign of calm in Darren's turbulent twenty-two hours in Barcelona, though he still needed his shades to stop the sunlight pinging off the white crockery and stabbing him in the retina, and his hand shook when he tried to butter the croissant. Claire watched Darren's slow return to life in partial sympathy – she'd had a rough night too, acting as nursemaid. The next step to recovery was a constructive conversation about their day, but this seemed a little ambitious for the present.

Nick smirked as he spotted Claire and Darren sitting like still lives out on the terrace. He made his way across, whistling jovially. Darren's head didn't move. Nick reached down and lowered the sun-glasses down Darren's nose.

'Dear, oh dear! Eyes like a three-month-old potato!'

Darren said nothing while Nick and Claire swapped jibes about his unfortunate night.

'It was stress!' he exclaimed suddenly. Nick sat down and opened a file. He'd been out and about early, picking up papers and forms for Darren's banking arrangements. Darren became irritable at the sheer number of signatures he had to provide, then swallowed his anger.

'Sorry. I had about three hours' sleep last night. I'd probably bite the head off Mother Teresa at the moment. And I still have to get used to the idea that I won't be going home in a fortnight.'

Claire and Nick shared a suffering look. Claire stood up decisively.

'The quicker we find somewhere to live the better then. C'mon, I'll make us an appointment with an estate agent.'

Darren wanted a quiet day, sitting still in the shade. House-hunting did not appeal. Perhaps Nick could help Claire out?

'Sorry, other things to do.'

'Mr Brown?'

Young frowned, startled by Darren's powers to recall after destroying so many brain-cells overnight.

'The guy who phoned you last night,' prompted Darren.

'No, I put him on hold. Time-waster. Right – catch you for lunch later, maybe?'

Getting no reply, Nick made his way off the terrace, then turned.

'Oh, and don't forget to tell the *Hello* mob!'

Darren slumped in his chair. Flat-hunting was bad enough, but doing it with a reporter and a photographer watching your every move seemed like writing a suicide note on your relationship. Fortunately, Darren was rendered so impassive by the dehydration gripping his body that he'd all but decided to let Claire make the choice of property. They were only renting, after all.

After rejecting a large flat in an apartment block with a view of another apartment block, they moved up onto the slopes above the city, now covered with a patchwork of modern suburbs and eighteenth-century villages.

In the Sant Gervasi district, Claire found a smart modern villa, done in eighteenth-century style, with garden and pool. She liked it, and Jasper and Lindy of *Hello* liked it too. Once Darren had given the nod, Jasper got weaving, taking pictures of the happy couple in their new home. Darren even took off his sun-glasses in celebration.

They returned to their hotel, and while Darren caught up on sleep, Claire took her latest Frances Fyfield novel down to the lobby for a quiet read. Until she was spotted by Lindy, that is.

'Strong woman character to your taste, eh? Mind if I mention your reading habits in my piece?' Claire gave her a dubious look. 'Look, if we'd wanted to take the piss out of you, would we be paying good money? Besides, the magazine doesn't operate by inviting the readers to sneer.'

Claire relented. 'Do you want a coffee, beer, wine?'

Lindy sat down and asked for a black coffee. Claire signalled a waiter and ordered two coffees in Spanish. Lindy purred. 'My, you have been busy!'

'I just "Berlitzed" my way through a few phrases, that's all. We'll both need to take proper lessons.'

'Most of the Spaniards I've met seem keen to speak English . . . well, American at least.'

The conversation began to flow beyond the realms of books and kitchen furniture, with Claire telling Lindy of her fledgling fashion career, and rather shyly showing her the 'Claire Travis' label inside her jacket. Lindy was impressed.

'You're not just here to clean Darren's football boots, are you?' she asked conspiratorially.

'I'm a beginner really. If it hadn't been for Darren, I'd have packed up. He rented a shop for me, gave me some money to get some designs made up . . . encouraged me.'

'Very enlightened of him! I thought most footballers chained their women to the cooker or the bedroom?'

Claire smiled and shook her head. 'I think Darren's different, in a quiet way. Must have been quite tough for him to break ranks from the "bunch of lads" way a football team thinks.'

Lindy was drinking this in, hoping she'd remember it all for her piece. The precise wording didn't matter – who remembers what they actually said each day? – but the general drift was clear. Claire thought Darren stood out from the crowd, and that he respected her own career and identity within the relationship, blah, blah, blah – perfect 'New Man' guff for the readers, who would be able to draw their own conclusions, thank you very much. Lindy had her doubts about Darren – all right, the poor bastard had a prize hangover – but there was something she couldn't quite believe with him. Nothing specific. Just a feeling that he was one of those blokes – and she'd known a few in her time – who couldn't be trusted. Lindy didn't dream of confiding this to Claire, of course.

The next morning, Jasper and Lindy shipped out, sharing a cab to the airport with Nick. He urged a note of caution in the feature.

'I'd go easy on the happy couple stuff if I was you. I think Claire'll be back inside two months. There's nothing out here for the likes of her!'

Lindy offered him a bet. Nick shook his head – he never gambled. And then he asked to divert the cab to the Princess Sofia Hotel. He had one last meeting to take which he'd almost forgotten. And 'No,' his look said to Lindy, 'this one is definitely private.'

'You're slippery too,' Lindy thought as she watched Nick scuttle into the five-star hotel, just a short walk from Nou Camp Stadium . . .

Chapter Four

Darren and Claire could hardly believe they were on their own at last. The media circus had packed up its tent and moved on. Nick had nothing else to do now except collect his commission by bank transfer. They were free of manipulators, doctors, club officials, intrusive journalists and rabid fans – and boy did it feel good.

They struck out on a late-afternoon stroll in an attempt both to celebrate their new-found solitude and to get a feel for the city that was now their home. Walking, if it was safe, was often the best way to find out how such a great sprawl as Barcelona functioned. And this nineteenth-century part of the city was easy to navigate, with the wide boulevards, flanked by elegant stone apartment blocks, crossing west-to-east, and the narrower roads fed commuter traffic either down south to the Gothic area and port, or north to the smart modern suburbs set in the hills.

It was now a Saturday, and the city was alive with the bustle of family groups enjoying their weekend and young couples buying clothes. Because the shops closed in the afternoon and then reopened from 5 until maybe 8 or 9 p.m., there was a sense of having two days inside one. You could feel the renewal of energy which the 'siesta' granted.

Within twenty minutes, Claire had found the Ramblas, the long, winding street which ran right down the heart of the city linking the smartest shopping areas of the Gracia district and the old port area, revitalised by the development for the Olympics. In between were places of night-time danger – the dark, narrow passages where pushers, prostitutes and junkies met in fatal embraces – and in front of them now, the vibrant stretch down from Placa Catalunya which was part café, part street-theatre, part market. Mime-artists, jugglers and buskers were everywhere; waiters scurried across through the single-lane traffic to deliver coffees and beers to customers sitting out in the late-afternoon sun; and traders offered jewellery, souvenirs, pets from make-shift stalls.

It was all a far cry from the sterile, shopping-mall blandness of his home-town. There, families retreated to their houses by six on Saturdays, with little better to do than cut the grass or slump in front of satellite TV, and perhaps a car-boot sale to look forward to on Sunday mornings. But here in Barcelona, Darren could feel the restless quest for spectacle, for activity, for celebrating life.

As they walked hand-in-hand, both Claire and Darren were aware that he was being recognised every so often – his paler-than-Spanish skin and fair hair would have attracted the odd gaze anyway. He had little chance of anonymity with his photographs adorning the assorted newspapers and sports magazines that hung in the kiosks on the Ramblas.

Darren found that the fans were content with a smile or a shy '*Hola*'. They seemed cautious about him, perhaps not certain what this new star in their midst was like. Perhaps they just respected his right to walk down the street.

'I've found a lady who'll give us Spanish lessons,'

Claire announced, distracting Darren from his thoughts.

'Wasn't a card in a phone-box job was it? Could be another service altogether,' said Darren, realising instantly that this was a crass remark, the sort of back reference to English life which he'd have to drop in order to appreciate Barcelona properly. Claire smiled at him patiently as he gave her a chastened look.

'She's the widow of a former British consul here. So she understands not jut the language but all the *un*spoken rules.'

'Great. We'll book up soon as we get moved in.'

'I have done already. We start next Friday.'

Darren stopped and gave Claire an admiring look; her powers of organisation were impressive. While he'd been falling around drunk and forgetting to bring any money, she'd sorted it all – house, currency, language tuition.

'I'd have been lost here without you, wouldn't I?'

Claire shrugged off the compliment. 'Bah! You'd have muddled through in the end.'

Darren nodded. Muddle was the right word where he and arrangements were concerned.

'I think part of the problem is that I have to concentrate so hard while I'm *on* the pitch, that my brain goes into neutral when I'm off it.'

Claire smiled at him, closing one eye beadily.

'Sounds like a great way of getting people to do things for you . . .'

Darren put his arms around her waist and pulled her close.

'I'm glad we've been left alone now . . .' They moved together for a kiss. Their lips had just touched when Darren became aware of two boys at his side in red and blue Barcelona shirts, speaking his name . . . 'Dah-Ran Ma-Chus'.

Two autographs soon became twenty, and Claire and Darren were obliged to take their leave of the well-meaning crowd of onlookers who gathered. It hadn't been unpleasant, as when complete strangers in English streets had sometimes abused him, but it was a clear reminder that footballers were the highest-profile people in Barcelona, and that he would have to measure his public life with discretion.

Claire and Darren had dinner – no octopus, but plenty of delicious fish – back at the hotel, then went up and sat on the balcony of their room with a bottle of white wine from the mini-bar. The sun was dropping behind the mountains now, but the air was still thick and warm. From the streets below the endless rumble of the traffic wafted up, mixed in with the thump of hip-hop music from a nearby bar, and the chatter and laughter from the pavement cafés.

Claire and Darren smiled at one another, they both liked what they'd seen and felt and heard – a city where it was good to be young and to have a bit of money to spend.

Darren's hand snaked out and cupped Claire's right breast through her shirt, stroking it gently almost as though he was collecting peanuts from a dish. Claire melted instantly. All the frantic activity of the last week had blocked out their desire for each other. Now with peace and privacy available, it raged up in them.

They scrabbled at each other's clothes, pulling and twisting at buttons and zips which felt like road-blocks. Within a minute, there was a tangled pile of trousers, knickers, shirts, socks spread across the floor, and the two bodies were free to express themselves. Darren put his hands under Claire's bottom and lifted her up. She clung to him as they moved across to the bed, kissing his neck and tonguing his ear. And then she heard him say he'd forgotten to bring condoms – another prime

70

example of his organisational chaos. Claire paused only momentarily.

'I'm too late in my cycle for anything untoward to happen. Besides, be nice to work without a net for once . . ."

They fell onto the bed and let the warm air and street noise accompany them in their rapture.

Darren stirred to the sound of church bells and the muffled 'whoosh' of the shower. And now the phone was trilling. Or was he still asleep? No, the phone really was ringing. Sunlight shafted in through the window. Darren blinked – Barcelona. I'm in Barca-bloody-lona! He grabbed the phone.

'Hello . . . I mean, *hola. Nick!* No, it's all right – I think we're an hour ahead here, aren't we?' The banter died in an instant. Nick was asking if Claire was there, in a firm and angry voice. 'No . . . She's in the shower, why?' Darren mumbled, sensing something amiss. Now, down the phone, through the cables and relays, came the news, all the way from good old England.

'Just listen,' Nick said emphatically. 'You have been turned over in a big way in the *News of the World*. Some bird called Jane who worked in Claire's shop claims you were tupping her, and that you've now deserted her and pissed off to Spain . . .'

Darren's stomach felt like it had flipped over. A terrible dread sickened him from his gills to his feet. Still the voice kept coming.

'Look, I'm not one to moralise, Darren, but couldn't you have found someone a little further from your own doorstep?'

Darren fell back on the bed. The noise of the shower had stopped. He tucked the phone into a gap between the two pillows.

'All right, all right. How bad is it?'

Claire came out of the bathroom in a towelling robe,

71

and lay next to him, kissing his neck. Darren covered the mouthpiece.

'It's Nick – pissing down in England, apparently . . .'

Claire shouted a cheerful 'Hi' before going across to the wardrobe. Darren listened as Nick supplied further details: the headline read 'Jane's Pain as Soccer Rat Darren Leaves for Spain'; there was a photo of Jane in a swimsuit, designed to show off her attributes. And there was also the photo of Darren and Claire taken at the airport.

There they were, kissing each other with sombreros on their heads and the toy donkey cradled in between them. Five million readers would be looking at it that morning – some would think, 'Good on yer, son, fill your boots, you lucky bastard'; others would call Jane a bitch or, less likely, Claire; and maybe most of them would think Darren a swine, who deserved this kind of slap in the face for all his success. Darren tried desperately to block out the enormity of events being relayed down the line. It was like someone trying to set off an atomic bomb in the safe, cosy, privacy of the room in which he and Claire had just expressed so much love for each other.

'Right,' Nick droned on. 'I'll do what I can damage-limitation wise, but you'd better be ready for a follow-up from the heavy mob. In the meantime, I reckon you've got maybe a morning to equalise it with Claire. Call me when you can . . .'

Darren put the phone down, hurting in the deepest pit of his stomach. Christ, he'd been an idiot. But then what a cow Jane must be. She'd waited just for the right moment to stick it to him. And poor Claire – what on earth could he do about her? He lay on the bed in silence for several moments, wishing he could rewind the world.

*   *   *

By the time he'd showered and dressed, Darren had at least decided that he must tell Claire but that he would try and delay it for a few hours. Not to spare himself from her reaction, but to give himself the chance to find the words of explanation he knew would be needed, and perhaps, just as importantly, their tone. There would be no good saying sorry if it wasn't sincere. He also needed to brace himself for the real prospect of Claire ditching him and going back home. On balance, he feared that's what she'd do.

To buy time and to escape the hotel were priorities. The other tabloid news-desks would probably be following up the story if they felt they could get a few days' mileage out of it. Sitting in the hotel room waiting for them to ring or, worse, to turn up, would just be playing their game. So Darren picked Tibidabo out of one of the guide-books in the hotel lobby. It was one of the major hills which overlooked the city and the views back down to the Mediterranean were supposed to be spectacular. There was also an amusement park up there, and a bar, and almost certainly no English Sunday papers.

Claire readily agreed to the excursion, seeing it as a welcome change of routine from their normal Sundays in England: lunch at Alfredo's, then back to the flat for sleep and telly. She also felt wondrously happy – their love-making the previous night had been more emotionally intense than ever before. It was as though they had been liberated from their long-established, routine personalities and allowed to see each other afresh again, capturing that first thrill of mutual attraction while retaining the depth they had already acquired.

The taxi ride up to Tibidabo took about half an hour, pulling up through the modern apartment blocks and shopping areas which had been part of the city's more recent expansion, and then out beyond the new ring road and up onto a twisting mountain road. At every turn in the road Darren and Claire could see the city skyline framed by the deep blue of the sea; the Olympic village towers, and spires of la Sagrada Familia, gradually faded into the heat haze.

The funfair was in full throng, packed with families and day-trippers, and teenage couples on dates. Claire took it all in greedily. But Darren was dying inside. Being surrounded by fun and laughter made it even harder to contemplate dropping his bombshell into Claire's life. He began to wish-fulfil that the affair with Jane hadn't happened, that England couldn't reach out and mess with his life now. He'd almost convinced himself that this was the case when he caught sight of Terry Corden, the *Daily Mail* journalist who'd been at the press conference at the club. Corden was hanging around by the gate, monitoring arrivals and departures. Fortunately Claire didn't spot him, she was busy wrestling with a *butifarra*, the Catalan version of a hotdog, sold from a stall inside the park.

Since it was impossible to eat this with elegance, Claire's hands had become sticky. She tossed the remains of the snack to Darren with a giggle, and went off to wash her hands. Now, bizarrely, Corden pounced, coming in quickly through the gate. Darren steeled himself.

'Go on, stick the knife in.'

Corden shrugged. 'I came to *warn* you, Darren. The Rotters are on their way out this afternoon.' Darren nodded in defeat – the term covered those journalists, mainly news but sometimes sports, who specialised in scandals and their follow-ups. They mostly hunted in packs, like hyenas, feeding off the dead carcass of somebody else's initial kill. Darren didn't have Corden down as one of them, but being out in Spain, he was in pole position to lead the attack.

'If you want to come and stay at our place for a few days . . .'

Darren gave him a sneer.

'So you can do a *little* exclusive?'

Corden spread his arms plaintively.

'Darren – I'm a sports writer not a shite-hawk! That's what I told the desk when they phoned!'

Darren lowered his head. Corden's motives were apparently sound. He'd insisted on his right to privacy on his holiday with the Master of the Hounds on the news-desk, and then tried to find Darren at the hotel, when Tibidabo was revealed by the hotel clerk.

'Sorry,' said Darren.

'You can lie low! If the rat-pack get nothing after a few days they'll be hauled back home by the accounts boys!'

'But if they can't get me or Claire they'll be swarming all over the club!'

'What are you going to do then, Darren?'

Darren kept one eye on the washrooms for a sign of Claire. 'I have to tell her soon as I get back to the hotel . . .'

'About the *Rotters*!'

Darren shrugged. 'After what Claire and I have got to go through, who cares, Terry?'

Corden looked at him with pity.

'They'll slaughter you, son.'

In the background Claire reappeared from the public toilets. Corden pushed a piece of paper into Darren's shirt pocket.

'My number – if you need it.' He scuttled away, not looking at Claire in case it embroiled him in a conversation he didn't want to have.

'Who was that?' asked Claire, almost remembering the face.

'Autograph hunter . . .' Darren looked at her gravely. 'Look, we should get back to the hotel.' He put an arm round her shoulders as he escorted her back towards the gate. She knew there was something wrong, but had not the slightest inkling of what devastation awaited her.

Darren waited until they'd reached the privacy of their hotel room, sat Claire down on the bed, and tried in as controlled a fashion as possible to tell her what he'd done and what the public consequences now were.

As he spoke Darren could see the colour draining from Claire's face. Then the frown. And finally the tears. Great shoals of them cascaded down her cheeks, dripping uncontrollably onto the bed. Her nose began to run. For fully five minutes she virtually turned to water before his eyes. Darren cried too, of course, but it was triggered more by the hurt he felt for Claire than for himself. In fact he felt detached from himself. Almost spectating from across the room as his exorcism took place. Finally Claire managed to blurt out the first of the many questions that had seemed tangled up in her vocal cords.

'But why *her*? Did it give you extra pleasure knowing I trusted her?'

Darren spoke quietly, frightened to look at her.

'It happened because she was easy – and I was weak. It wasn't done to hurt you.'

'Well it bloody well has. I feel so *stupid*! So humiliated!'

Claire's voice was getting stronger now, louder, angrier. Darren tried to quell the impending storm.

'If it's any consolation I *had* finished it. That's why

76

she blabbed to the press. Revenge. For me leaving, closing the shop down. It was her who slashed the tyres on my car . . .'

'You shit! You must have promised her something for her to do that. Was she on the short-list for Spain as well as me?'

Darren looked into Claire's tear-filled eyes.

'There was never any chance of that,' he said firmly, relieved to find a truth he could utter. 'Believe me. It was just a bit of . . . not even fun . . . shagging, that's the only word for it.'

'Doesn't say much for our sex-life then, does it?'

'I dunno what it says. It's like those people who shop-lift then can't remember why they did it . . . that's how little it meant to me.'

There was a generality here, and a rationalisation which sounded alarm bells for Claire.

'Sounds like there's been others then?'

Darren stayed mute, hoping the silence would be confessional enough.

'Are we talking hundreds?'

Darren snorted.

'No! They were just part of life on the road with the team. Hotel waitresses, barmaids . . . shows you how pathetic they must have been to see someone like me as glamorous.'

That tipped Claire right over – she didn't want to hear any self-pity from him.

'Don't be so condescending you asshole of a man!' she shouted. 'I'm supposed to take consolation from the fact that you slept with nobodies? What do you think that makes me feel like?'

Darren had no answer. Even the ringing of the tele-phone provided no escape. He knew who it would be by now.

'Don't answer – it'll be the press.'

He took the telephone off the hook, replaced it, then took it off the hook again to block the line.

'I think you should get out of here, 'cos there'll be a lot of shit flying around. Do you want me to ring the estate agent to see if you can get into the house tonight?'

'Don't bother,' Claire snapped.

Now there was a loud knocking at the door. And then a male voice. English. No-nonsense.

'Darren! It's Barry Huddleston from *Today*. I wondered if I could have a word with you. You know, set the record straight. Darren?'

He knocked again. Darren stood up.

'I'm gonna have to go out and face these bastards. Just stay put and don't answer the phone or the door. Okay?'

Claire managed a nod as she wiped more snot from her nose with the back of her hand. She looked just like a little girl who'd fallen over in the playground and grazed her knees. Darren made his way to the door, making to touch her, but then thinking better of it. As he went out, Claire heard the first few yelps from the press boys waiting outside.

Darren insisted that they get as far away from the room as possible. So he led the pack down to the lobby and found a chair in a corner, backed up against the wall. He wanted them where he could see them – in front of him, in a group, with no one whispering deals in his ear. He didn't even try to identify them. Most of them were unfamiliar faces anyway. Well-fed, podgy, and shiny – from life on a higher level of expenses no doubt.

The tape-recorders were soon thrust into his face as the pack settled. Darren wanted this over in one go. So he'd let them all have their kicks until they were sated. The questions were fired in from all angles.

Darren looked straight ahead and answered in a matter-of-fact monotone.

'How do you think this might affect your future with Barcelona?'

'I don't know. I hope they'll see that it's something that was purely to do with being in England.'

'Won't it raise doubts about your character for them?'

'Maybe. All I can say is that I'm not married, and that it won't happen again.'

'How's your girlfriend taken the news?'

The monotone disappeared. 'How do you think, pillock?'

'Must have been a bit of shock for her?'

Darren held up his hands to get some breathing space.

'Hang on – you manage to make it sound like she just heard this through idle gossip. Some of your colleagues *paid out* money to get this woman to shop me! It was a wilful act of malice!'

This was dangerous, fighting back. The more he did that, the harder they'd bite.

'You *are* a public figure, Darren . . .'

'Yeah, a footballer. Not a politician, or a civil servant or a copper!'

Out came the sanctimony which only the truly cynical can call upon.

'But you're a hero to many kids . . . your professional standards come into this.'

'Oh, gimme a break! I did wrong, I know. But the only person I'm accountable to is my girlfriend, and that's a private matter between us. Okay?'

Some chance. They scented another kill.

'Can we talk to . . . Claire, is it?'

Darren shrugged. 'That's up to her.'

'This girl back in England says she slashed the tyres

79

of your car in revenge – are you worried that you might be in a "Fatal Attraction" situation?'

Darren hung his head in silence. There was nothing he could say that wouldn't sound frivolous or offensive. And any silence would draw out their impatience. Soon they were on to the next question. And the next. And the next . . .

When there was nothing left to answer, when he'd finally bowed to their desire for his public humiliation, the hunters drifted away to confer and to start writing up their copy. No doubt some would try and get on to the club, but they'd be pushed on a Sunday. Darren hoped that having gorged themselves on him, they might leave Claire alone. He went back to the room, drained and haggard.

Claire, in contrast, had gained control of herself. Her face was washed, and she'd also changed her clothes. Nothing was said. Darren leafed through the room-service menu.

'Do you want something to eat?'

'No, thanks.'

'Omelette, or burger maybe? You'll faint other-wise.'

Claire shook her head. She seemed abnormally composed. Maybe she was on her way home. He didn't dare ask.

'Would you rather I found another room?'

'We have to sort a couple of things out,' Claire said, applying make-up now.

'Right. I do love you, you know. I won't make it out here without you.'

Claire looked in the mirror to catch his eye.

'*Please* – if you wouldn't mind putting *my* feelings first for once.'

'Sorry.'

'Since we're in the business of opening each other's

guts up, I may as well tell you that I've had a couple of flings of my own over the years.'

Darren was too bleached out to react. He could barely feel anything any more, so numbed was he by the turmoil.

'Oh. Right. Can I ask who with?'

'You can ask, but I'm not telling. It was nobody special. Nobody who'd go to the papers about it either. Just somebody who was around to care when you weren't and didn't.'

'Was it anybody I know?'

Claire snorted with contempt. 'I doubt it. It was nobody to do with football, for sure.'

'Right. I suppose all this is down to us getting together too young? Not living enough beforehand.'

It was a plea for mutual sympathy. For a peace-treaty. But Claire seemed cold and detached.

'Maybe for you. The other problem we have is to do with what we did last night. Would you do me the courtesy of having an AIDS test?'

Darren blinked at her.

'I know it's unlikely – or then again, maybe it isn't – but I have the right to know, don't you think?'

'I had one during the medical the other day. Result should be through later this week.'

Claire gave him a killing smile.

'Well maybe they knew something about footballers that I didn't!'

The evening and the night seemed endless. They barely spoke to one another as Claire installed herself in front of the TV and watched American films dubbed into Spanish. Darren risked a trip to the bar but retreated when he glimpsed the press pack guzzling in self-celebration. He ate the scraps from the mini-bar – peanuts, corn chips – and a couple of apples from the fruit bowl. In truth he felt as though his stomach had shrivelled. Then Claire moved the beds apart, twenty-four hours after she'd pushed them together. She went to sleep quickly. Darren watched her for hours wondering if the hurt could ever be cured. He slugged back a few brandies but they gave him nothing but a headache. Eventually he fell asleep in the chair.

The usual morning call from Nick woke him. Claire was nowhere to be seen.

'Believe me, Darren – these ain't too bad!' he chirrupped down the phone, rustling through the papers. 'They're all basically saying the same thing – that you were a bit naughty and had a leg-over with a girl your fiancée knew! There's nothing more they can say – unless she gets pregnant or tops herself!'

Nick was missing the point, of course, but Darren didn't have the energy to tell him. He just lay the phone on one side. He could still hear Nick droning on.

'So I'd advise against pressing charges for the damage to your car. And I'll call Gamez for you and warn him about things, just in case. Now get on with the job and stay calm . . .'

Darren looked at the phone, it seemed to have an abstract life of its own with its faint Cockney voice. What a clever phone it was!

'Now, there is just one more thing. Because they've already got pole position as it were, the *Hello* people would like a few more words with you about this new turn-up. Just so it fits with the pictures, right . . . Darren? *Darren?*'

Darren stuffed the phone under a pillow and turned over. He wasn't sure if he fell fully asleep again but when his eyes opened Claire was in the room; showered, dressed, face clear of make-up, but also dry of tears. She held out several sheets of notepaper. Darren could make out big letter-headings in familiar type-faces.

'I seem to have had a lot of post shoved under the door in the night. Offers ranging from five to fifteen thousand for my side of the story.'

Darren lay there on his stomach, head turned to watch her.

'What are you going to do, take the money and run?'

'You really think I'd play their game?' Claire binned the letterheads. Darren felt a sudden surge of reassurance. Nothing to do with being spared more shit in the press. More to do with the fact that Claire seemed herself again – strong, decisive. A conversation seemed possible for the first time in over thirty hours.

'Look – I've got to go down to the stadium and be introduced to the team later. Do you want to meet up this evening, maybe?'

Claire didn't look at him. 'I'll see.'

Darren took a breath – it had to be asked.

'You're not going home, are you?'

'I don't know yet.'

'Look – I finished it. I knew it was wrong. I wanted this to be our new start . . .' said Darren, repeating his mantra of mitigation.

'Good luck with the team,' Claire said passionlessly, before heading for the door.

'There's a fire exit on the right. Go down that way!' Darren cautioned. Claire didn't even turn.

'It's not me they're after, Darren . . .'

Just how true this was hit Darren as his taxi arrived at the main gates to the Nou Camp Stadium. The same gaggle of English press, now augmented by photographers, clamoured round the black and yellow cab. A couple of club stewards forced a passage through and the taxi sped up to the main entrance, where Gamez paced, looking thunderous. He wagged his finger at Darren as he moved into the club.

'It's a good thing that Nick telephoned to warn me! They are like animals!'

'I'm sorry about this. Really,' Darren pleaded. He hadn't expected them to get at him via the club but the cost of the trip meant that they had to come back with more than just one scalp.

Gamez led Darren down a staircase and into the cool concrete-lined corridor which led to the dressing-room areas.

'The President is most disappointed with you, Darren. Today, he organises for the supporters and the press to meet the team and the new coach. And what does he get? A mob of paparazzi interested in your sex-life!'

Darren couldn't grovel enough. The thought of this poison spreading into his new life overwhelmed him.

'I had no idea . . . it was something from the past, a last bit of England . . .'

Gamez scowled at him. 'Well I hope there's no more to come!'

He opened a door and from the gloom of the corridor they moved into the bright, warm light of the huge dressing-room. Darren gawped at the luxury – spa bath, plunge pool, hooks hung with sumptuous bath-robes, slip-on sandals under each changing bench, massage tables. Most of the Barcelona first-team squad were already in the room, some changed into the new season kit. The chattering stopped as Darren was ushered forward by Gamez who introduced him in Spanish. Darren saw their looks, weighing him, trying to work out what manner of dick-head he must be to provoke a press binge on the club's photo-call day.

'*Buenos dias, senores!*' Darren managed before faltering. 'Sorry about the English journalists. My fault!'

Gamez headed for the door, ordering them to be

ready in half an hour. Darren shuffled awkwardly. His Spanish was limited, but even if he'd been fluent, he'd have had trouble overcoming the embarrassment. Then the tall Number 6 wandered over, holding out a hand of welcome.

'Darren, hello. I am Manuel Utrillo. Captain of F.C. Barcelona. Come and meet the team . . .'

Relief surged through Darren, not just because Utrillo spoke English, but because even though the other players jabbered at him in Spanish, they were plainly welcoming him. Utrillo shouted names and nicknames as Darren moved through the room, then pushed him across to where two contrasting types stood. Darren recognised them from the few Barca – he would soon get used to calling the club by its diminutive – games he had seen on satellite TV. The tall guy was the attacking Dutch midfielder, Wim Cuipers and his smaller companion was the team's 'play-maker', the Dane, Jesper Petersen. They both spoke good English.

'We've been hearing about your exploits, Darren,' Cuipers said with a wide grin.

'It's a bit surprising that only *one* girl can cause so many journalists to follow you . . . in Denmark, you would have needed a dozen!'

Darren was grateful for their good-humour. It couldn't make good the official displeasure he would no doubt face, but it reassured him that this dressing-room, like the one he'd known so well back home, was a sanctuary for the players, where no outside forces were allowed to penetrate.

'What will the local press make of me?' Darren asked.

'They bite here too,' Petersen said with a shrug. 'But only if your sex-life means that you play badly.'

'Just my luck to be English!' Darren said ruefully.

Utrillo reappeared and dangled a red and blue Barca

shirt in front of Darren. He swirled it round to reveal a number 9, and the name 'Matthews' in white letters across the shoulders.

'*Delantero centro* . . . centre-forward!' Utrillo said with a smile, but the number didn't need any translation. The realisation that this was his shirt meant more in that instant to Darren than the contracts and the money and the boot deals. He was about to join a revered institution, and here was the symbol of belonging. The poignancy of the moment was interrupted by the strutting arrival of the tall, dark-haired goalkeeper Jesus Vila, dressed still in black denims and T-shirt, with a number of gold chains hanging from his neck. The first image shouted 'playboy' to Darren, but Cuipers put further spin on it when Vila offered Darren a palm to slap.

'*Hola, Darren – Soy Jesus Vila – el portero!*'

'But his main position is team lunatic!'

Vila held a finger for a pause, then turned on Cuipers and pushed him right back across the tiled floor and into the plunge-pool. Laughter went up all round the room, and Vila returned to collect 'high-fives' from as many colleagues as possible.

He came back to Darren and out of his mouth came English with a mid-Atlantic accent. This fitted in with the impression Darren was building of Vila's world – night-clubs, discos, 'chicks', movies – but the cultural mix had more surprises.

'Darren, I will call you "Stanley", okay? Because of "Matthews", okay?'

Darren shook his head and laughed. But Vila hadn't finished.

'Now listen to my English which my friend Gary Lineker gave to me! When referee gives penalty against me, I say . . .' Vila mimed an outraged hands-on-hips stance, 'Kinnell!'

The players were cracking up at the goalkeeper's antics, even though they'd seen them all before.

'Kinnell, ref!' Vila grinned. '*Bueno, hey?*'

Before he could say any more, Cuipers pounced from behind and draped his soaking wet shirt over Vila's face. Whatever was going on outside with the press, or upstairs in the official rooms, Darren at least felt he belonged in this not-so-little corner of the Nou Camp Stadium.

The players duly put on their new season kit and boots, and Utrillo led the squad out of the dressing-room, down into the tunnel, past the players' chapel (that was an eye-opener for Darren) and then up the steep steps which brought them out onto the edge of the pitch.

Darren hadn't seen the stadium at playing level, but as he mounted the steps and the great bowl came into view he felt he understood what the Christians must have felt coming out to face the lions. Even though the ceremony was no more than a photo-call for the team and the new coach, there were still five or ten thousand supporters in the stadium, waving the red and yellow flag of Catalonia, or the *blaugrana*, the emblem of Barca.

The squad lined up on the edge of the pitch facing up to the Presidential box. The club's committee were installed and Vaqueras made his way down to a podium, decked with microphones. Darren took another look around and then froze . . . there in the Presidential box was Nick Young. He'd mentioned nothing about coming out that morning. Darren's mind raced – Vaqueras must have summoned him to discuss penalising Darren over the scandal. Maybe Darren was 'on his bike' already without kicking a ball in anger?

The tannoy played the Barca song, and out of the crowd came the noise of drums being beaten along

87

with the tune. When the rousing chorus had finished, Vaqueras leant into the microphones and began his speech – in Catalan, as tradition required. Darren listened intently, but the language defeated him; it was like Spanish and French had been magimixed with baby-talk. Fortunately, Vila was standing next to him in the line-up and was able to offer some translation.

'He's signed a new tough-guy coach . . .'

'Who is it?' begged Darren. Vila shushed him as the speech went on.

'This is the usual stuff about discipline and effort . . .' Vila passed on. Then he stiffened.

'English!'

'What?'

'He says the man is English!'

Before Darren could react, he now saw the familiar head of Kenny Dawes, manager of the English Premier League Champions rising into view up the steps. Kenny Dawes – the new coach! Darren looked up at Nick Young, trying to catch his eye. Nick shrugged. Dawes was giving a double-handed wave to the crowd.

'Kinnell, hey, Stanley!' Vila said with a nudge.

'Yeah, very much Kinnell . . .' Darren replied, mindful not only of Dawes's favoured style of play, but also of his opinion that he didn't rate Darren. Just the kind of new boss he wanted!

Dawes mounted the podium, shook hands with Vaqueras, and then approached the microphones. Making no concessions to his new environment Dawes began to boom out a speech that might have made sense in Manchester, but almost certainly didn't in Barcelona.

'Mr President, supporters of Barcelona! This is a great honour! Now here are two promises – this year we will win the League Championship again! We will also wallop Real Madrid whenever we come across them!'

Vila leant in on Darren. 'Wallop? What is this, Stanley?'

Darren just shook his head in dismay.

Later the players were invited up to the committee room, to take drinks with their new boss. But first of all Darren wanted to get at the truth of Nick Young's involvement. Nick saw him coming and knew what was on Darren's mind – those calls from a mysterious 'Mr Brown'.

'All I did was handle some of the negotiating for him. And I couldn't let on to you, with things so finely balanced. Vaqueras wanted to ace Gamez – he'd got an English centre-forward, so the President had to go one better!'

Darren hung his head. 'All this way to be coached by Kenny Dawes.' Darren made no attempt to change his hangdog expression, even as Dawes approached him. He patted Darren on the shoulder matily.

'Well you look suitably gob-smacked!' he smiled, misinterpreting Darren's mood.

'I'm entitled to be, aren't I, "Mr Brown"? After what you told Nick here. What was I – "a one season wonder"?'

'Darren! That's in the past,' Dawes said, blandly. 'Besides, this game's too full of opinions that don't matter. All that matters now is that you and I make a good job of it, eh?'

'Provided I make your team . . .' said Darren, fishing.

The matey smile on Dawes's face vanished. 'That's up to you, isn't it? I mean, sounds like the President's got the hump with you over shagging this bird, so let's not give him any more excuses to make me drop you. At least I'll knock you off the sports pages – ought to be grateful for that!'

Dawes wandered away introducing himself to the

other members of the squad. God knows what they must have thought of this sudden English invasion.

'He wouldn't have signed me though, would he? Given the choice?' Darren asked Nick.

'No,' Nick said, truthfully, 'but he's got you. So prove him wrong!'

Darren sipped his drink wondering if the move to Barcelona had any more surprises for him. Then he felt a hand on his elbow. He turned. It was the club doctor.

'Darren . . . a word, please. I have the results of your HIV test . . .'

When Darren got back to the hotel, he found that Claire had checked out. There was a note though – 'Gone home'. Darren winced. Then it occurred to him what she might mean by 'home'. Darren took a taxi up to the house they had planned to rent. He got no answer from the front door. But making his way round the side to where the pool was, he found Claire sitting, face tilted into the late-afternoon sun. He watched her for a moment.

'Do I take it you're staying?'

She shielded her eyes and stared at him.

'If I give up now, I'll probably spend my life wondering what might have happened. Besides, I've got things I'd like to achieve out here.'

'Sure,' said Darren. He put a tentative hand on her bare shoulder. Seconds later she kissed it gently. There was still some passion left, despite all the treachery. If they worked at it, their relationship stood a chance. Whether either of them really wanted that, only time would tell. There was nothing more to be said for the moment – all the anger and the fear had been spent. They drifted into a perfectly banal conversation about Darren's day, and promptly stumbled into a terrifying misunderstanding. When Darren referred to a nasty shock, Claire was alarmed to think that he might have been declared HIV positive . . . but the doctor had given Darren the all-clear. The nasty shock was five feet ten, stocky, loud-mouthed and called Kenny Dawes . . .

It took only a few minutes of the first training session for Dawes to let the rest of the Barca squad know what Darren meant.

'Keep it *simple*! Play *hard*! Knock it *long*!' was his personal credo, shouted out to the bewildered players who stood like bedraggled dogs as a midsummer shower soaked them through. Darren watched the grey clouds gather round the mountains in the distance and wondered if he'd ever be allowed to leave England behind.

Chapter Five

It didn't take Darren too long to cement himself in the affections of the Barca fans – thirty-two minutes to be precise, for that was when he scored his first goal for the club in their opening League game of the season against Cadiz. Utrillo had broken up a Cadiz attack and then hit an instant long-ball over the halfway line for Darren to chase. The explosive speed over five yards that Darren used to get his goals inside the penalty-box, at least took him clear of his marker, but the Cadiz sweeper came across to cut off his run. Darren feinted to go inside the defender then went outside and drilled a low shot past the keeper from the edge of the penalty area.

The Barca fans stood to cheer this auspicious start to the Englishman's career, and Darren indulged in a little continental display, kissing the badge on his shirt as a symbol of his new commitment. He was genuinely excited. Only when he found himself interviewed on the touchline at halftime by Radio Catalan, did he realise that it had been seen as '*un gol tipico Ingles*' by the reporter.

'*Espero que non es el ultimo,*' replied Darren, hoping to piece together sufficient Spanish words to make a sentence. What he meant was that it wouldn't be the last he scored, but it probably sounded like a warning that there were more 'English goals' to come. For while

Darren had done his best to settle at the club, the intrusion of Kenny Dawes had altered all his preconceptions. Quite simply, he found himself living in a fantastic city, playing for one of the Continent's finest clubs, but being coached as though he was a centre-forward for a Sunday-morning team on Hackney Marshes.

Dawes reduced the game to its basics: defend tight, hit the ball long, shoot on sight. The idea of building up a move involving dozens of passes, of giving an individual the chance to use his talent, of using patience and subtlety simply did not appeal to Dawes. He'd been a tough-tackling wing-half in his playing days of the late 1960s, a work-horse, and he'd carried this ethic through into his managerial career, with considerable success. Winning the English championship had made all his fancy-pants critics howl, and he had the trophy to prove how effective his methods could be. He plainly saw no point in changing his style for Barcelona. After all, that's what Vaqueras had bought, hadn't he?

In the dressing-room at halftime, Dawes reminded his players what he wanted from them, although his colloquial, north country English threatened to defeat the club official who acted as translator. The gist became obvious anyway – always look for the chance to hit Darren with a long ball. At this, Darren mimed an exhausted runner, only half in jest. But soon Dawes retaliated with a mimic of his own. Trying to urge his team to avoid 'typical Spanish fanny-merchant football', he was reduced to mincing around the dressing-room to get the message across. It amused Vila anyway.

Less funny was the way the team played in the second half. Their spontaneity had gone, probably because they were too aware of following Dawes's instructions. And when Utrillo took the tight-marking of a Cadiz forward too literally, he found himself flat-footed when a pass came over his head for a Cadiz midfield player to run onto. Utrillo and his fellow defenders gave chase, but to no avail. Vila was beaten by a clever chipped shot – 1–1!

The atmosphere in the stadium fell flat. Barca, confused by the new tactics, simply couldn't find the invention to fight back. The players trooped into the dressing-room at the end knowing that something was wrong but were too unsure of themselves to speak up. It was only the first game, after all.

Darren at least had the consolation of his goal to cheer him, and toured the dressing-room enquiring where 'the lads' normally went for a drink after the game. It emerged that this wasn't the Spanish way; most of the team simply went home, or had a late dinner with their families. The idea of the English 'wind-down' – a few drinks, maybe a disco – hadn't got through to them, except of course for Vila, for whom football seemed to be a minor diversion compared to partying.

Eventually a party of four – Darren, Vila, Cuipers and Petersen – made their way across to the Princess Sofia Hotel for a post-match drink. Claire, who'd insisted on coming to see Darren's first match, found herself tagging along, with Nick Young as escort. This uneasy gathering acquired additional tension when Kenny Dawes wandered in. He was staying at the hotel until such time as he found a house, although a five-star hotel, with room service, bars, swimming-pool and rich women coming and going probably suited him better.

For the players, who'd already been muttering about the team's tactics, Dawes was an unwelcome presence – not that Dawes would have ever noticed, such was his self-confidence. Claire, however, had quickly worked out that as the only woman in the group, she would be surplus to requirements for the next few hours. Darren, torn between being one of the boys and being his own man, dithered as they discussed plans. Claire put him out of his misery by asking for the car keys and disappearing. Darren did nothing to stop her.

The six men made their way out onto the Gran Via outside the hotel, and called up a couple of taxis from the waiting rank. Barcelona was full of discos and bars, designed to the hilt with hi-tech facilities, but the place they wanted was one in which they could give Kenny Dawes the slip most easily. Happily their first choice fitted the bill.

The disco featured an entire wall of video screens, which projected images over the dance-floor, and a first-floor bar from which non-groovers could watch the action, or size up the man or woman of their choice. Dawes waded straight into the centre of the floor and went into a dance routine so old it might well have been back in fashion.

The players watched from the balcony above, waiting for the chance to disperse into the night without offending their new boss.

'He dances as though they've got a ball and he's going to tackle them!' Petersen observed as Dawes moved in on a group of young women dancing together. Nick Young came up from the dance-floor, unable to go Dawes's pace, and slumped into a seat next to Darren.

'Look, why don't you guys move off and I'll look after him?'

Vila promptly stood up to accept the offer.

'Let's go – we can introduce "Stanley" to *las pijas*!'

'Who are they?' Darren asked.

'You'll see,' said Cuipers with a knowing smirk. They finished their drinks and set off for the exit, assuming it could be found in the general bombardment of visual images. Nick took hold of Darren's elbow and shouted in his ear: 'Don't play too strong, Darren. I can't market an English yobbo in Spain, it's not very original.'

Darren nodded. He understood the warning. Any more bad publicity after the Jane affair would probably sink his career. He followed the others out. Nick leant over the balcony; Dawes's frenzied frugging had cleared a space on the dance-floor. It was going to be a long night.

The players' next port of call was a bar high up on the slopes above the city, with a dazzling view of the city at dusk. Spanish rock music blasted out, and the cars parked outside – BMWs, Mercedes, Porsches – suggested the bar was some way short of being a clip-joint. Vila led the party in, plainly enjoying the instant attention which was a Barca footballer's natural environment. He found a space overlooking the floodlit garden, signalled for champagne and, almost within seconds, he and his team-mates were surrounded by a group of very good-looking, immaculately fashionable young women.

'*Las pijas* are the daughters of the rich, Darren,' Petersen explained.

'Shouldn't they be buying the drinks, then?' Darren joked. In reality, he was knocked sideways. Sure, foot-ballers in England could turn a few heads in their town's local disco, but these women looked like they'd stepped out of the fashion pages of *Vogue*. As Vila held court, Darren found himself catching eyes with one of the girls on the fringes of the group. She smiled at him. Cuipers put an arm round Darren's shoulder.

'This area's called Tibadabo. From the Temptations of Christ. When Satan took him to a high place and showed him the world . . . *Haec Omnia Tibi Dabo* . . .'

Darren looked at Cuipers with a frown. Was that Catalan, and what did it mean? It was Latin. 'All these things I will give you . . .'

Darren looked back at the girl. She gave him another flashing, confident smile, a pure come-on. And he felt temptation rising within him. Perhaps he should just stay a little longer . . .

Two hours later, the four players and six of the *pijas* were drinking in a vast penthouse apartment, lined with modern art and sculptures. The haunting voice of Catalan singer Joan Manuel Serrat drawled out of the most expensive stereo unit Darren had ever seen. Vila was dancing, locked in an embrace with one of the *pijas*, while Darren sat alongside the girl who had been eyeing him up. All he knew about her was that her name was Eva, she was beautiful, rich enough to own this flat, and probably not as old as her clothes and manner suggested. He was trying to find out more, but Eva seemed more interested in Darren.

'Where did you live in London?' she asked, her English giving no traces of a Spanish accent.

'I didn't. I'm not from there. There's other cities, you know,' Darren burbled, unnerved by her scrutiny.

'I lived in London for two years,' Eva said airily.

Must have been an au pair, or something, Darren thought, but didn't say. 'What were you doing then – you know, as work?'

'My father owns a publishing company. I was in London just to see the museums and art galleries. I do the same here.'

Darren was beginning to get the picture. A girl with serious wealth and lots of time on her hands – couldn't have put it better if he'd gone to a dating agency. Not that he was planning anything untoward. Claire was back home tucked up in bed alone, and Nick's warning echoed ever louder in his mind. No harm in having a little flirt, though.

'Don't suppose you watch football, do you?'

'Maybe now that I have *met* you, yes . . .'

98

Darren could barely contain himself. Her dad was probably a millionaire, and she was *interested* in him! They talked more, for an hour or so, and Darren was pretty sure he didn't mention Claire once.

Eventually, the party broke up around 4 a.m. Darren and Petersen were the first to leave after it became obvious – well to Darren, at least – that there was no question of sex on a first date or anything like that. Vila and Cuipers hung on, just in case there was more to it than a civilised evening of drinking and talking.

Outside the apartment block, the streets of the city were quiet for once. Petersen led Darren back towards a main thoroughfare to try and pick up a taxi.

'Sorry it was a goalless draw, Darren. The trouble with some of the *pijas* is that they only like to flirt. Sleeping with a footballer would be just a joke for them.'

'I can think of worse ways of having a laugh!' Darren said with a smile. They reached the wide strip of the Diagonal, one of the great boulevards crossing the city. Taxis were stacked up at a rank. Petersen and Darren crossed towards them.

'This is your first time playing abroad, isn't it, Darren?' Petersen asked, although he'd guessed already that the Englishman had little experience of living abroad.

'Yeah, one-club man before that.'

'So enjoy it, Darren. At thirty, people like you and I are finished with football. There's plenty of time for a boring life afterwards.'

Darren nodded. It was the last thing he wanted to hear. Encouragement to dive in and sample everything that was on offer didn't quite square with what Darren was trying to achieve. But as he climbed into the taxi, to be greeted by an ecstatic driver talking him through his goal of the night before, Darren had a nagging feeling that Barcelona's temptations might prove stronger than his own willpower.

Stumbling round in the kitchen in the dark while he made himself a jam sandwich, Darren was surprised by Claire. She came over and leant into him, pressing close. Her body was warm from the bed. It was a gesture of apology for going off in a huff. Darren responded with his own.

'I'm sorry. I didn't *know* Nick and Dawes were going to turn it into a "boys' night out".'

'I suppose I should have guessed and stayed away. Where did you go?'

Darren was in mid-bite fortunately, and so had time to find the right neutral phrase.

'Thrashed around a few of those designer bars, that's all. Just looking, you know?'

'You sure?' Claire probed sleepily. 'Macho *is* a Spanish word. What happened to Nick?'

'Went off with Dawes somewhere . . .'

'Why wouldn't he stay with us?'

Darren shrugged, even though he knew the answer.

'Might have felt he was intruding. Maybe he didn't want to embarrass us by bringing back some floosie to bonk?'

Claire stretched herself. 'We should take advantage of his discretion.' She held out a hand to take him back to bed.

'Hang on, I'm all jammy,' Darren protested.

Claire began to lick round his mouth. 'Story of your life . . .'

When Darren woke at about 10.30, the first thing he became aware of was a rich, male Spanish voice somewhere in the house. He went out onto the landing. The voice was coming from one of the spare rooms. Darren pushed the door open. The room had been transformed overnight into a makeshift studio, with

Claire sitting behind a drawing board, sketching out a few designs. On the window-ledge stood a cassette-player, playing a language tape. Claire leant across and switched it off.

'Thought for a moment you had Julio Iglesias in here! What gives?'

'Just thought I'd get back into the swing of things. Might as well see if I can get some work out here.'

'I'd have thought design was a bit of a crowded market in Barcelona,' Darren said beadily, leaving the room. Maybe it was the lack of sleep, but the thought of Claire getting on with her own little plans irritated him intensely. He had no right to be angry, because at heart he wanted her to *do* something with her life rather than just be a classic football wife, 'looking after the home'. After he'd showered and dressed for a meeting in town with Nick, Darren isolated what was eating into him – it was the prospect of Claire succeeding.

Nick hadn't needed to be too busy marketing Darren to the Catalan public. The very fact that he'd signed for Barcelona made the Englishman a highly desired commodity for sponsorship or endorsement deals. Nick had already scored him a Mercedes 300 from one of the city's main dealers. This morning's package involved a proposed clothing tie-up with one of Spain's leading department stores, although Darren had yet to catch sight of the 'schmutter', as he called it.

'Trust me!' urged Nick as the Spanish businessmen left with their autographed photos of Darren for their sons. Nick poured out more coffee as they sat back and enjoyed the sunlight on this terrace café just off the Ramblas. Business couldn't be easier, thought Nick as he stretched and yawned.

'How did you get on with Kenny?' enquired Darren. Nick closed his eyes as if trying to shut out painful memories. 'The man's a complete slut. I'm afraid I had to come down to his level.' Nick opened one eye. After a moment, Darren twigged.

'You paid for it?'

Nick shrugged. 'They were class tarts, Darren! Tattoos spelt correctly and all that! Besides, I can put them down as business expenses. How about you and the lads?'

Darren relayed the story of his night, and the teasing encounter with Eva. Nick was impressed by the idea of her social connections. If he could tap into that kind of market, well . . . !

'You know, if you were out here unencumbered, as it were, you could have all that. Sex, high society . . .'

'I'm supposed to be making a fresh start with Claire . . .' Darren pleaded.

'Listen, Claire's out here for herself. Don't be in any doubt about that. The good life – with you paying the bills.'

This didn't square with reality, but the less than subtle hint about Claire's own agenda added to Darren's unease about the role she was playing in his life, and he in hers. The tension over this came to a head after their first joint language lesson with the old lady who'd been a consul's wife. She was a game old sort, and had even picked up on the press criticism of Barca's English-style play in the opening game, so the introductory chat had gone smoothly enough.

But then Claire had hi-jacked the proceedings, suggesting a lesson to fit in with her plan to take designs around Barcelona's fashion houses. If that hadn't been bad enough, Senora Trobado, the tutor, pronounced herself 'in' with the fashion-designer set, and offered to introduce Claire to her friend, Rafael Jiminez, one of Barcelona's most successful designers. Claire had been thrilled, Darren less so. Once outside, he let rip.

102

'How the hell will "hello, this is my portfolio" come in handy on the football pitch?'

Claire shrugged him off, she was too excited by the prospect of a good contact to get dragged into a row with Darren. But he was spoiling for one.

'*I'm* the one who's got to work out here!'

'What am I supposed to do? Sit at home all day with the odd trip to the supermarket as light relief?'

'There was never much chance of that by the look of it,' said Darren sarcastically.

'What's that supposed to mean?' Claire snapped.

'That you're set up already!'

'I'm only trying to work for my living. If I spent my day wandering round art galleries, you wouldn't think very much of me, would you?'

Darren fell silent, not because he was lost for a reply, but because Claire's remark had brought someone else to mind. Eva.

The Barca training pitch was situated to one side of the stadium itself, flanked by the large car-park which ringed Nou Camp, and a small, grassy viewing area where fans could gather and watch their heroes hone their skills. When the players emerged from the stadium changing-room and crossed to the practice pitch for the first session since the Cadiz game, they assumed that an over-eager fan had been at work. The plastic traffic cones used in dribbling and passing exercises had been deployed to cordon off the four corners of the pitch, angling out from the six-yard box to the touchline. Vila, hitching a ride on Darren's back, reacted first.

'Kinnell, Stanley! *Que pasa?*' Darren could only frown. He suspected Kenny Dawes was up to something, and so it proved when the team captain, Utrillo, challenged him with a curt Spanish phrase.

103

'What's he gassing on about?' Dawes asked. Nobody dared answer – Darren thought he'd heard the words for 'circus' and 'dogs', but wasn't about to pass that on.

'I think Manuel just wants to know what all this is for, boss . . .' Darren offered.

'Well if he asks in the English I know he speaks, I'll tell him!'

Darren suffered. He was hardly a stunning linguist, but by showing himself willing to learn he'd eased his way into the workings of the squad a lot quicker than if he'd played the little Englander. But how could he tell his boss that he was in danger of becoming one?

'With respect, boss . . . it's *his* country!'

Dawes glared at him fiercely. 'I don't give a shit about whose land it is, Darren! This isn't Cowboys and bleedin' Indians! I just want my job to be made easier! Now let's get on with it!'

He clapped his hands and gestured for the players to gather round. 'Okay – now normally, on a motorway, traffic cones tell you where *not* to go! Today, however, is different!'

Somewhat reluctantly, Utrillo began to translate for the non-English speakers in the squad as Dawes moved across to one of the lines of cones.

'We will be trying to play the ball *into* these corners! Because when you get back onto your home pitch in there, you will find that the grass is *longer* there than elsewhere! And that means we can hit balls into the corners without them skidding out of play! Understand?'

Not many did. Darren guessed that Dawes was pulling one of those stunts that some English league clubs had tried from time to time – narrowing pitches, over-watering the grass, that sort of thing. Longer grass in each corner was the trademark of several clubs who relied on the long-ball game for their success. So much for a level playing field, thought Darren.

The squad began to take up positions for the practice match, and as Dawes put the ball into play and blew his whistle, there were a few moments of stifled hilarity, before Utrillo sarcastically booted a huge pass towards the farthest corner of the pitch and Darren set off in among the cones. He stretched to control the ball then wellied an ambitious shot towards goal but way over the bar. Dawes blew his whistle and advanced on Darren.

'If I didn't know any better, I'd say you were taking the piss, Darren!'

'I'm not Marco Van Basten, boss,' Darren said with a shrug, the Dutchman being, in his prime, one of the few players who could score from such an acute angle. Dawes glowered.

'The idea is: we knock the ball in behind them; they're turning and we're not. If you win it in that sort of position, Darren, you look inside for our runners . . .' Dawes's gaze fell upon Cuipers and Petersen, '. . . who should be on the edge of the blee-din' box by then!'

Utrillo strode out towards Dawes spreading his arms in exasperation.

'This is now like a game of golf, not football!'

Dawes smiled. 'We are looking for the same in-gredients. Not just the right range of pass, but also the angle! Just like Sevvy Ballesteros and Olaza-what's-his-face . . .'

'Olazabal,' Utrillo corrected, pointedly. 'You don't understand, I was making the criticism. This kind of trick is illegal!'

'Bollocks!' Dawes exploded. 'Clubs all over the world are at it – anything which might suit their style of play!'

'But our grass is perfect! We were meant to be a passing team!'

The row was becoming more heated now. Dawes could lip it with the best, but Utrillo's comments seemed to him like downright mutiny.

'The old coach has gone now – the new kid is in town!' Dawes said thumping his own chest proudly.

'Not for long,' Utrillo muttered as he walked away.

Dawes chased after him. 'Was that a threat, sunbeam? Eh? Eh?'

'How could it be? You are a man who doesn't even *listen* to his players!'

The ironic logic was lost on Dawes. All he saw was an uppity Spaniard who would have to be told who was boss. The rest of the training session was played out in a thoroughly poisonous atmosphere.

At the end, the players retreated to the trestle-table on which bottled water was provided and a mutinous muttering continued while Dawes busied himself getting the traffic cones collected. Utrillo took Darren to one side and tried to persuade him to have a word with Dawes, on the basis that he might listen to complaints from his compatriot. Darren was dubious about this.

'He may be my countryman, skipper, but he's still the boss. I've got no right to approach him.'

'But all this shit with the cones and longer grass. It's not the way the game should be played. It must be stopped!'

Darren shrugged. 'Well, you must know about the power structure in the club – from what I see the President and Vice-President have a big say in the running of the team. Vaqueras brought in Dawes, Gamez brought in me. Can't they be used to put pressure on him?'

'Only when we lose!'

'Well, I'm not happy about what Dawes is doing, but I'm damned if I'm going to play to lose!'

'Exactly, so, please, can you not have a word with the boss? Take him for a drink, tell him how we feel?'

Darren shook his head emphatically.

'Where I come from, that's not done, Manuel. The workers and the management don't get together.'

Utrillo looked disappointed. He tossed his empty water bottle into a plastic bin.

'I think, Darren, that you must decide whether you are here in Catalonia or still back in England!'

Darren sagged. He could see how he could end up torn apart if the squad's relationship with Dawes continued to sour. If he tried to talk to him, he'd probably get bollocked and dropped from the team. If he said nothing, the players would see him as being too loyal to Dawes, and ostracise him.

Darren left the stadium in a reflective mood, signing a few autographs for the fans waiting by the main entrance. He stiffened as he heard Dawes's voice calling him from behind. Dawes gestured for him to come back inside the building.

'I'm just off, boss.'

Dawes approached. 'Do you fancy a drink tonight?'

Darren shrivelled inside. Going out with Dawes but not being able to say anything relevant to him seemed just about the worst option in the circumstances.

'Er, can't manage it, I'm afraid,' Darren said unconvincingly.

'Maybe later in the week then?'

'Sure. I'll see what I can arrange.'

Dawes gave a pathetic little smile. 'The hotel walls are moving in on me a bit. Is Nick still around?'

I bet I know what you're after, thought Darren. 'No, he's down in Madrid, lining up some fashion deals for me.'

Dawes chuckled. 'Being paid for what you wear! What a game! You worked out what to do with your afternoons yet?'

'Not really. Feet haven't touched the ground yet.'

'I'll find us a golf club,' Dawes said decisively. 'Top of the range! Least I can do while I'm out here is get my handicap down!'

Damn it – Darren was almost beginning to feel sorry for the man. Maybe he was vulnerable, after all.

'Boss . . .'

'Yeah?' Dawes's face was alive with expectation, hoping perhaps that Darren might suggest an afternoon with four hookers as recreation.

'Some of the lads are worried about this long-ball game.'

Dawes's face became a mask again. He gestured to the ground. 'There is an invisible line down there . . . between work and play.'

Darren recognised the tone and backed off.

'Invisible, eh? No wonder I couldn't see it. Sorry.'

Dawes stared into his eyes to check the level of sincerity. Darren began to blink, but the moment was broken by the arrival of an open-topped sports saloon, horn tooting for attention. They both turned. Eva sat behind the wheel, wearing shorts and an expensive polo shirt. She waved to Darren. A smirk began to spread on Dawes's face.

'I thought you said you had nothing sorted . . .'

Darren crossed to the car, and found himself being invited to accompany Eva to the Barcelonetta, the old port area, refurbished before the Olympics. With Dawes watching, he could hardly chicken out. Besides, if he went home, Claire was bound to be working on her bloody designs. Darren nodded and climbed in. Worse things had happened to him than being driven round Barcelona by a beautiful woman in an open-topped sports car.

They parked the car by the harbour, and set off along the Passeig Nacional, one side of which formed the harbour wall, the other being an endless row of smart seafood restaurants. During the drive, Darren had been able to note Eva's *pija* accessories – the gold Lady Rolex, the designer clutch-bag, the silver bracelets, Armani sun-glasses. She probably had designer under-wear, but Darren stopped himself from thinking too much about that.

'I've been asking some of my male friends about you.' Eva announced as they walked.

'And?'

'They tell me that the team is changing its play to suit you.'

Darren shook his head, smiling. There was no escaping the football intrigue in this city. It was probably way ahead of sex and politics as a topic of discussion. But rumours had to be stopped somewhere – here was good enough. Eva was probably on first-name terms with the club's hierarchy anyway.

'It's not true,' said Darren patiently. 'The coach is changing the play, and it suits neither me nor the team. Tell your friends that. I expect some of them might know the President?'

Eva's smile gave nothing away. 'What do you think of my city?' she asked, turning to take in the sweep of the harbour, overlooked by the rugged crag of Montjuic and the seventeenth-century façade of the old port buildings.

'It's terrific. Don't know how much I'll get to see of it though . . .'

'I can be your guide,' Eva volunteered.

'To all the expensive bits,' Darren joked, only to find himself topped.

'*We* don't see them as expensive . . .'

Darren felt a first tinge of irritation or what, if he was honest, was the deep-rooted male instinct which recognised a 'prick-teaser' at work on his emotions.

'Look, Eva, why did you turn up like this?'

'You left without leaving a number,' she said bluntly.

Darren shrugged. 'I didn't know I was expected to stay in touch.'

'Well now you do. I'd like you to come to lunch tomorrow. Just a small party.'

'Is this a single invite?' Darren asked, trying to clarify her intentions.

Eva smiled beguilingly. 'That's up to you. You know my address . . .'

The conversation didn't go much further. Eva announced she had another appointment. She dropped Darren back at the club and sped off saying simply 'See you tomorrow'. Darren couldn't figure her out. She obviously liked him, but wasn't sure it amounted to anything. He'd seen quite a few large groups of young men and women at restaurants in Barcelona and, thinking like an Englishman, had assumed they were all 'at it'. The more he'd seen, however, the more it reminded him of an American TV series set in the early sixties – all high-school proms and soda parties. There was an innocence, a chasteness about it which he didn't really understand. Probably something to do with Catholicism. He'd have to take up Eva's invitation to find out if it applied to her.

Back at the house, he found Claire breast-stroking her way up and down the pool. When she spotted him watching her, she swam over.

'I haven't been doing this all day, if that's what you're thinking.'

Darren smiled. 'Listen, I'm beginning to see how life can work out here. Relax.'

'Wish I could,' Claire said tetchily. Darren touched her arm. 'What's up?'

Claire pulled herself out of the pool and lolled onto Darren. He didn't mind – the sensation of warm water soaking through his shirt was thoroughly arousing.

'I got knocked back by three fashion houses today. They wouldn't even see me.'

'I told you not to mention my name,' Darren added, self-mockingly.

'Not the greatest of starts.'

Darren caressed her back, unable to stifle a slight feeling of pleasure at her failure.

'Cheer up,' he suggested vacuously. 'Look, I've invited a few of the lads over with their wives on Wednesday night. Try and widen our circle a bit, eh?'

Claire couldn't see how this would help her at all. She didn't want to end up stuck in a circle of un-employed soccer widows, taking coffee with one another every day and moaning about how their hus-bands were never at home.

'Sure,' she said unconvincingly. 'One snag though . . .'

'It's okay,' Darren said anticipating the objection, 'I'm not going to invite Kenny Dawes.'

'We have other guests arriving . . .'

Darren frowned.

'Your mum phoned. They're coming out tomorrow night.'

'*Tomorrow?*' exclaimed Darren, heart sinking at the prospect of a parental visit so soon. Their unique ability to churn up his emotions was exactly what he didn't need right now. He and Claire were still bruised, he had his relationship with Dawes to sort out, and now Eva was an added complication. Why couldn't they have waited till they were invited?

111

'Some free flight deal for buying a microwave oven, apparently,' Claire explained.

Darren stood up, water-stains all over his clothes. 'Well, I hope they bring it with them so I can stick my head in it!'

Chapter Six

Kenny Dawes thought it would be a nice, quiet day at the stadium, having put down the players' mini-revolt – another training session in the morning, done his way. Spot of lunch, then a round of golf at his new club, before putting in an hour or two back at the office. A Spanish-style working day. He'd just changed into his tracksuit, collected his clipboard and stopwatch – sprints told him more about a player's fitness than anything else – and was about to make the short walk across to the training pitch, when he ran smack into the club President, Vaqueras. There he was, standing outside his office – at 9.30 in the morning.

'Mr President! Good morning . . . *bonas* . . . *bieno* . . .' he said, struggling to keep his nerve.

'A moment, Kenny,' Vaqueras said quietly.

'Sure. Shoot, as we say!'

Vaqueras didn't smile. Maybe the joke didn't travel. Maybe he wasn't in a laughing mood.

'I'm sure this is a misunderstanding . . . but about the pitch. There can be no tampering with it.'

'Tampering?' Dawes asked innocently.

Vaqueras walked into the room, claiming an unspoken sovereignty over it. 'Changing it to our advantage. This is not the Barca way. We want to win, but not by underhand methods.'

Now that he knew the game was up, Dawes thought

he may as well try and justify himself. 'With respect, Senor President, we ought to try for every benefit our home stadium can give us.'

Vaqueras held up his hand with finality. 'But not this. I insist.' Dawes saw that he meant business. He thought about an apology, then decided it would show too much deference. 'I'm surprised you misjudge the spirit of the club so badly,' Vaqueras added.

Now it was time for an apology. 'A beginner's mistake . . .' Dawes said with a shrug.

'Which would not have happened if you had consulted me first.'

Vaqueras left without a further word. Talk about putting a marker down. This was a neon-lit sign telling Dawes who had the real power at the club, on and off the pitch. Four weeks, that's all it had taken for the reality to set in. Dawes had suspected it all along. This wasn't like England where you could bamboozle a chairman with tactical talks, get him to cough up money for transfers he didn't know about, sweet-talk him, bully him, make him look a dick-head in the press. But this bugger Vaqueras was into everything – he was a successful businessman, he spoke English, he was sharp, and what was worst, he was elected by the bloody supporters!

Dawes stomped all the way to the training ground, head jutting out. If he couldn't control the President, he would certainly make sure that he controlled the players.

One of them, and he couldn't avoid the pun, had 'grassed' him up over the pitch, and whoever it was would get their card well and truly marked. Prime suspect was Darren.

Dawes separated him from the rest of the players who were chatting in a group.

'Was it you, Darren? Eh, eh?'

114

'Me what?'

'Somebody shopped me!'

Darren frowned in bewilderment. Dawes rounded on the rest of the squad. 'When I find out who it was, he'll be lucky to get a game for Real Nintendo! Right!' he barked. 'Because my game-plan has been scuppered, you lot will find yourself having to put even *more* running into every match! So off you go – ten laps of the pitch! Tell 'em, Darren!'

'*Diez vueltas, tipos!*' Darren muttered. But they'd already got the message.

After training, the players went their separate ways, grateful at least that the traffic cones had had their day. Darren left with Vila, checking whether he was bringing his wife to the party at Darren's house.

'No way, Jose!' Vila spluttered. 'I thought you would provide the girls.'

'It's not that sort of party, Chus.'

'Well, we'd better find some this afternoon then!' The goalie was incorrigible. Darren shook his head and headed for his car. He had a busy day ahead: parents arriving, lot of shopping to do, and he thought he might at least drop in at Eva's lunch party. Just for a look.

When Darren arrived at her apartment, he was the first guest. Or so he thought. Then he saw the table laid out on the balcony – there were only two chairs.

'I thought other people were coming?'

'They cancelled,' she said blandly. 'Wine?'

Without waiting for an answer, she disappeared into the kitchen. Darren took in the apartment again. Probably not much change out of £400,000, he guessed. And then there was all the art. Seconds later Eva appeared with a tray bearing wine, glasses and a huge lobster salad. He didn't imagine she'd prepared it herself. Probably given the butler a half-day off. Darren

115

scratched his head. This was fantasy time – the city stretched out through the windows, the sun was shining, and he was having an intimate little lunch with a beautiful, rich woman. Bit of a step up from judging the wet T-shirt competition in a disco back home. But Darren was unsettled.

'Look, Eva . . .'

She was sitting at the table, pouring wine into his glass, confident he would stay. That was probably the reason he felt unnerved. *He* was being 'hunted'. He also thought he'd put all his philandering behind him. But this would be tough to turn down. He could almost hear his mates back home shouting 'Go on, my son! Fill your boots!' Then he thought again – maybe she just wants to talk . . .

Darren and Eva went to bed immediately after lunch. The sun and the wine had doused any doubts in Darren's mind, and there were obviously none in his body. She allowed him to undress her, slowly, almost inviting him to see the designer labels. He fumbled with the catch on her bra.

'Sorry, I've never been very good with these . . . what are they called here anyway?' he wittered nervously. '*La brasero*, or something?'

Eva laughed. 'That is a barbecue.' She slipped the silk brassiere off herself. 'This is called *un sosten* . . .' She took his right hand and placed it on her left breast. '*El seno* . . .' Now she leant forward to kiss him. '*Un beso* . . .' Darren wrapped her in his arms and lowered her tenderly onto the bed.

Two hours later he was cruising out to the airport, with the top down on the Mercedes and one of his favourite tracks on the stereo: 'Love is So Much Better When You're Stealing It' by Z. Z. Hill. It wasn't quite how he felt. He felt no relish at cheating on Claire again. The afternoon had just seemed like a dream,

116

a private fantasy come true. Something in a bubble almost.

But the moment his parents, Freddie and Lil, bustled out of the airport terminal, with their pale white skin and cheap holiday clothes, the bubble burst and vanished.

'You could bake to death in there,' Lil moaned, gesturing with contempt at what she saw as the greenhouse structure of the terminal. 'And that marble floor! I bet people go arse over tip when it's wet!' It felt like a long drive back to the house. And they were only warming up!

As Darren parked the car on the gravel drive and went round to the boot, he saw them look at the villa with bewilderment.

'Bloody hell, this must be Band bloody Z in the Council Tax!' Freddie exclaimed. Darren lugged their cases from the boot.

'I told you – we're only renting!' Even this didn't stop them.

'Rent?' asked Lil. 'I thought you were on top money here, Darren?'

Even the diplomatically spiced and sauced casserole of hake that Claire had prepared for them, eaten out on the terrace on a sunlit evening, couldn't get past the frontier posts of Lil and Freddie's terror at being abroad. Freddie spent most of the supper ostentatiously hoiking tiny fishbones from his mouth, while Lil took one look at the salad and sniffed.

'Amazing, isn't it? All this sunshine and they still turn out green tomatoes!'

When Freddie declined to taste the £25 bottle of vintage white Rioja, Darren waved the white flag.

'I'll take my dad out for a pint, if that's okay, Claire?'

Claire smiled in sympathy, while Freddie perked up in an instant.

117

Darren drove him down into the Barrio Gotic, the atmospheric fifteenth-century part of the city, which at night became a maze of ill-lit but enticing allies, dotted with bars and cafés and women of the night. He found a traditional tapas bar that Utrillo had mentioned to him, and proudly indicated the wide range of delicious snacks which were the stock-in-trade of these bars. Freddie peered into the refrigerated counter seeing all manner of unknown sea-food and animal body-parts.

'Looks like an aquarium!' he said squiffily.

'Come on, Dad!' Darren pleaded. 'Look at it – deep-fried, fresh squid; spicy sausages; king prawns; smoked country ham; anchovies; artichoke hearts. It's fantastic. Bit of a change from your average English pub – twenty variations on mince!'

Freddie gave him a grudging nod. They made an effort, he supposed, these Spaniards, he'd give them that. And the beer wasn't as bad as he thought it would be. He couldn't really begin to tell Darren how knotted up he felt. He'd never travelled, not through choice, but through basic poverty. And he was too late to enjoy it now that Darren could provide for them. He hated himself for being like this, especially when Darren seemed to have taken it all in his stride.

'You must have settled well if you're into this sort of thing,' Freddie observed.

'Long way to go yet,' Darren ventured tentatively, fearing more irritating comment if he sounded at all cocky. He shouldn't have worried.

'You were bloody lucky to survive what that girl said about you in the paper. Thought they might have put you on the first plane back.'

Darren controlled himself. 'Well, they're a bit more understanding about that sort of thing over here.'

'Oh, aye? Does that mean you're still spreading it around?'

Darren excused himself and went to the toilets. He thought about slipping away and leaving Freddie there, stuck in a strange bar in a medieval maze with no sense of geography and no language. Maybe he'd understand what it was like then.

Back at the house, Claire was scarcely having a better time. Lil had taken the men's departure as a cue for a heart-to-heart with Claire about the Jane affair and the publicity. This was the last thing Claire wanted – reopening her wounds for the inspection of strangers.

'I'd have left him if I were you,' Lil announced firmly. 'He can't have been right in the head to have gone with that girl . . . Girl? Trollop!'

'Well, things are never that simple, Lil. We've both been hurt by it. Hopefully we can put it behind us now. Anyway, Darren's doing well, that's the main thing.'

'*He's* got all the help though, hasn't he, love? Agent. Steady job. English manager. Fallen on his feet. Not like you.'

Claire was touched yet troubled by this. Lil was coming on like a feminist critic, and what's more she was basically right. But Claire thought she'd steer clear of discussing her own frustrated ambitions. A mother, even a feminist one, only really wants to talk about her son.

'It's still not that easy for him, Lil, the pressure's enormous.' Claire tried to change the one-way drift of the conversation. 'I mean, he's a bit confused as to why you didn't come out for a weekend, when there'd be a home match to see?'

Lil shifted uneasily on her seat. 'Look, promise you won't tell Darren – but we thought we might embarrass him if we turned up at the club."

Claire bit her lip and took Lil's hand reassuringly. 'You mustn't think that, Lil!'

119

In bed later, Darren and Claire swapped notes in a whisper.

'I wouldn't be surprised if they went back tomorrow morning,' said Claire.

'Christ, let's hope so. The thought of them being around for this party . . .' sighed Darren. Knowing what Lil had said, Claire tried to soften Darren's emotional spasm at their intrusion into his new life.

'Don't be too hard on them, Darren, this is all a bit much for them, I think.'

Across the hall, in one of the guest bedrooms, Lil and Freddie lay awake having their own whispered conversation.

'They're not happy. I can tell,' Lil said.

'I'm not surprised. Too much of a leap for them this. You need to be educated to live abroad.'

'I'm not looking forward to this party, are you?'

'Well, we'll do our best!' Freddie said defiantly. 'Try not to let them down.'

He turned on his side and held on to Lil.

'Must be bloody lonely here though. Everything's so strange. So unfamiliar.'

The omens for Darren and Claire's introductory party were established long before it started. Nick Young was just setting off for the villa from his hotel when he found himself joined at the taxi rank by Kenny Dawes, wearing one of his best white, Cecil Gee, suits.

'Wotcher!' Nick said cheerfully.

'I was just looking for you actually! Finished in Madrid?'

'Yeah – done a fabulous deal for Darren. Clothes for life. Shall we share a cab?' Nick offered.

'Sure,' said Dawes, grateful for Nick's company again. 'Where do you fancy?'

Nick wasn't quick enough on his feet. In fairness,

he'd been out of Barcelona and knew nothing of the row between Dawes and the players.

'I'm going over to Darren's,' he said, with a frown. 'For the party. You're coming, aren't you?'

Dawes covered up well – but then he was used to it. 'I've blanked it actually. Not my scene.'

The awkward moment was broken when a hotel doorman opened the door of the cab for them. 'No, no – we're going separate ways.'

Dawes watched with a patient smile as Nick climbed in and sped off. He would just have to make his own entertainment that night.

Claire had decided on a buffet by the pool for the party, to help people mingle and move around. It also avoided the tricky business of finding somewhere to seat Lil and Freddie. With a bit of luck, she and Darren would be able to steer them away from any possible embarrassments thrown up by the food, or the wine, or the language, or the culture.

Darren had invited his inner-circle friends within the squad, the English speakers who'd helped him settle in – Cuipers, Petersen and Vila. He'd also felt obliged to invite the captain Utrillo despite being told by Wim Cuipers that his wife Daniella was 'a bit of a ball-breaker', with an agenda ranging from sexual politics to a Marxist overthrow of the European Community.

While Claire laid out the food, Darren made sure everyone had a drink, then took Freddie and Lil around, under careful guard, to meet his friends and their wives. They negotiated the first stage successfully, with Vila even kissing Lil's hand for a laugh. But Darren made damn sure he emphasised the word 'captain' when he brought them across to the Utrillos.

'This is Manuel Utrillo, the club captain, and his wife . . . Daniella,' Darren said, with an arm round his mother's shoulders.

121

'I'll never remember all these names,' said Lil, flustered by the unfamiliar barrage of Wim, Jesper, Jesus and such.

'Manuel's easy enough,' chortled Freddie, unaware of the implied insult. Utrillo took it patiently.

'You must be very proud of Stanley, Mr Matthews?'

'Is that what you call him?' Freddie asked with a chuckle, astonished that the name of such a famous English footballer could have rippled out to such distant lands as Spain.

'It was the goalie's idea, Dad. And he's got the worst sense of humour in the team!' Darren smiled. So far so good.

'Is the manager not here, then? I thought he'd be only too happy to come, being English.'

They all tried to avoid the questioning look in Lil's eyes.

'He couldn't make it, Mum,' Darren said diplomatically.

'Out scouting probably,' Freddie guessed with a tone suggesting professional knowledge. The phrase certainly amused Nick Young.

'Almost certainly, Freddie!' he confirmed with relish, enjoying the thought of what Dawes would really be up to by now.

In fact, Dawes had settled for a modest start to his solo evening. He'd persuaded the taxi driver to try and find an English-style pub he'd read about, somewhere near the university campus, the City Arms. Dawes had been overjoyed when the premises loomed into view. But expecting a room packed full of exiles, eager to fête him with their attention, Dawes had been disappointed to find that although the pub was a more than authentic recreation, right down to the hand-pumps of English and Irish beers, it was actually full of young, denim-clad Catalan students for whom it was just a local.

Dawes propped himself up at the bar, sank a pint of Guinness and waited for his white suit and familiar face to pull in the crowds. Nothing happened. He tried another pint. Halfway through it, he heard a voice with an Irish accent.

'You're that Kenny Dawes, aren't you?'

Dawes turned to see a big, bearded Irishman, about thirty years old, wearing a check shirt and jeans, standing next to him. The Irishman offered a shovel of a hand to shake.

'Michael Hurley . . . Jack Charlton says you're a good feller and that's fine enough for me! Can I buy you a pint?'

Dawes shook hands with Hurley. 'That's very kind, Michael. Always got time for a fellow Brit.'

Like Utrillo, Hurley shrugged aside the unwitting insult and, speaking Spanish, ordered two more pints.

'So tell me – how are you adapting to Barcelona?'

Dawes leant closer and gave Hurley a confidential wink. 'It's a piece of piss, frankly! What you doing over here then, Michael?'

'I worked on the Olympic village site last year. Decided to stay on 'cos I like the city and the people so much.'

Dawes nodded sagely. 'Well, I suppose there's always work for labourers out here . . .'

Hurley gave him a curt smile. 'I'm a civil engineer actually.'

Even Dawes sensed a mistake this time. 'Oh, sorry. Just that with the shirt and the Guinness . . .'

Hurley made a point of giving Dawes's ice-cream white suit the once-over. 'We can't all dress the part . . .'

They gave each other thin smiles. They were stuck with one another for at least another pint and a half now.

Back at Darren and Claire's party, the guests had taken seats around the pool, balancing plates on their knees, and a vague circular discussion about Europe, prompted by Daniella Utrillo, had spluttered into life. Cuipers gave Darren an 'I told you so' look.

Daniella, a university lecturer in her late twenties, was very much a modern Spanish woman, having grown up in the heady spirit of freedom and personal growth which had gradually flourished after the dictator General Franco had died in 1975. The old days of sitting with the other wives in the back of a room, dressed in black, had never been her destiny and she celebrated that in her work.

'Come on, Darren, how do you explain why the English are such bad Europeans?' she asked, hoping to provoke more vigorous discussion. This was to be avoided at all costs as far as Darren was concerned, so his answer was deliberately frivolous.

'Let me see – I think it's because we play too many games and don't have enough time to work on our skills in training.'

Daniella frowned at him. Vila applauded from the sidelines. She was exactly the type of woman he hated. 'Good answer, Stanley!'

'I'm waiting for a *serious* one, Darren,' she persisted.

'You won't get it from me, English footballers aren't allowed to be political.'

He saw his mother about to speak – she'd back him up.

'You've got a brain, Darren. Speak up!'

Darren winced. Typical parental move – say the unexpected. All eyes were on him now. Darren struck out from the shore into deeper waters than he was used to.

'Er, well – if you want my opinion, I think most

124

English people feel isolated from Europe. Apart from holidays, that is.' He looked round for reactions. Freddie raised a finger.

'It's simpler than that, Darren. We won two World Wars. *So . . .*' Freddie shrugged. His argument was incontrovertible. Daniella sat forward.

'My God, what fascism! Relishing victory in war!'

Freddie bristled, searching for words. 'Please don't call *me* a fascist! I'll have you know that my uncle did a lot of work for refugees coming to England to escape your Civil War!'

Fatuous though the link was, Darren seemed impressed by this news, but his mother was now trying to control Freddie in a way that could only provoke him further.

'Give it a rest, Freddie.'

Freddie glowered at Lil. He wasn't going to come abroad for the first time and find himself and England accused of fascism. Britain had perfectly good reasons for its views on Europe as far as he was concerned.

'I'm just putting this lady right. Britain is an island nation, and you won't change the way people think with a tunnel!'

Freddie was pleased with this almost Churchillian salvo. Claire exchanged a look of foreboding with Darren. Sensing the tension, Nick sat forward and tried to calm the discussion.

'Wait a minute – I want to hear from Daniella, about how she sees the English. I suspect there's some misunderstanding on her part. Daniella?'

Daniella paused before launching into her assessment. 'You don't travel well and, if you do, you have a superior attitude; you cling to things from home – food and beer. Your country is run by useless, in-bred aristocrats and populated by aggressive peasants who eat terrible food.'

125

She looked across at Freddie. '*And*, you are always talking about the war . . .'

Nick laughed, even though it was obvious that she hadn't been joking. 'Dammit, she's right!' he shouted.

Freddie laid his plate aside, stood up and walked back into the house.

Darren sat back in his chair. The silence was as deep as the pool.

Meanwhile, Kenny Dawes's excursion into the unfamiliar territory called 'Mingling with the Public', was coming to a fraught close. He drained his pint and checked his watch. Ten-thirty. Things would be livening up now.

'Right, I'm off. If you fancy a bit of madness, Michael . . .' Dawes was only trying to be polite. So too was Hurley.

'No, no – this is fine for me.'

Dawes couldn't resist showing off, letting this buttoned-up, serious Irishman know that the English liked The Crack too.

'Only, I found a collection of really mucky women the other night. My treat, if you fancy one . . .'

Hurley had heard enough. He pushed himself away from the bar. 'Actually, Mr Dawes, I think men who have to buy women are pathetic bastards – see you around.'

Hurley left the pub. Dawes tried to hide his crushed pride. It was a good job there were no English in, after all . . .

These two separate but equally disastrous evenings had differing, but none the less profound effects on Darren, Claire and Kenny Dawes. Dawes found in his social isolation a reflection of all he had feared about the move to Spain. It was too much to expect a man of his age to change, so the Spanish, the Irish, the club, and especially the bloody players, would just have to take him as he came.

In contrast, Darren and Claire found themselves shivering at the thought of continuing a life abroad with closed minds. As they watched Freddie and Lil leave in their taxi for the airport and the eventual sanctuary of their England, they made separate vows to make the most of the opportunities this move had presented. For Darren, this meant confronting Dawes at the earliest opportunity about his simplistic tactics and blunt approach to a game which Barcelona, by tradition, had seen as a rich and complex form of entertainment. And as far as Claire was concerned, she simply had to get out and hustle if she wanted to achieve recognition for her work.

The weekend presented them all with the opportunity to turn their convictions into practical acts. Barca had an away game on Sunday against Osasuna, which meant a stay in a hotel on the Saturday in preparation. There might be time for Darren to catch Dawes in a mellow mood after dinner and sound him out regarding a change of style.

On the same day, Claire had been invited to a party at the home of their language tutor Senora Torbado. She had promised that her fashion designer friends would be there, providing Claire with an open goal as far as important contacts were concerned – if Claire could summon the self-confidence, that is.

Darren's opportunity came first. The players had settled into their country hotel, some twenty miles away from the Osasuna Stadium. Darren had found himself nominated as Vila's room-mate after an ambush by the rest of the squad, who plainly knew that sharing with the ebullient Lothario could be a tiring as well as a distracting business. But in his new spirit of determination, Darren took it in his stride. As the players spilled out into the gardens after lunch, Darren told Vila of his plans to tackle Dawes.

'You don't have to do this for us, Stanley,' Vila said, generously offering a cop-out.

'I'm doing it for myself as well, Chus.'

Darren watched Dawes flop into a sun-chair with a glass of wine in his hand and winked at Vila. The time had come. Darren strolled across to Dawes who, perhaps sensing yet another tedious act of bolshevism, looked straight ahead.

'Can I have a quick word, boss?'

' "Fast" – how's that?'

'Funny. Look . . .'

'How come you want my company now when it wasn't good enough for you the other night?' interrupted Dawes.

Darren shuffled uneasily. 'Look, I'm sorry. I couldn't invite you – I had half the team round.'

'So? I coach all of you.'

'Yeah, but it was the vocal half. Who don't fancy this long-ball game much.'

'I've told you, Darren – the invisible line. I wouldn't have brought work to a party.'

'But *they* would have. That's how it is here!'

'I've noticed! Treacherous bastards start squealing at the slightest provocation!'

Their voices were getting louder. Across the terrace Vila was busy circulating the news of Darren's attempted 'coup'.

'Well no, they won't . . . they wouldn't. If you treated them like adults . . .' Darren went on.

Dawes pulled at his ear-lobe with irritation. 'You're determined to have a pop at me, aren't you? If you think you're going to change my tactics by cutting me out of your social life, dream on, son! I can cope on my own!'

128

Darren wasn't going to give up now. He tried the personal, patriotic line, which he'd previously fought shy of, just in case it brought he and Dawes too close.

'Kenny – please. I just want to talk for a moment. Brit to Brit.'

'Why should I give you the time of day, Darren?'

'Because in the long run, I can save your job . . .'

Dawes nearly choked on his wine. This was cheek of a high order. He caught sight of the squad watching Darren and himself and stood up.

'Come on, away from here.'

Dawes walked Darren off the terrace and out into the hotel's tree-lined gardens. Once out of ear-shot of the rest of the squad, Dawes adopted an apparently softer tone.

'Now look, Darren. I know that sooner or later I'm going to get the sack here. The President's marked my card already – if I do what he says, I'm fine. But if I do my own thing and fail, then that seems better to me than *succeeding* on somebody else's terms! Do you get me?'

'Don't you think that's how *we* feel, the players?'

'Darren, *you're* paid to play, not to organise some kind of trade union! You're here now begging me to adapt and change my principles, when you lot won't even give my ideas a chance!'

'Yeah, but . . .'

'But nothing, Darren! I shouldn't even be talking to you!'

'But the fact that you are, is because we *are* in a different situation!'

Dawes stopped walking, making sure nobody had followed. 'Darren, these are "take the money and run" jobs, these. You can't just graft yourself onto a new country! You do what you can, while you can – if I can grab enough months over here to get a deep sun-tan, then some dumb chairman back home will rush to hire me 'cos he thinks I'm all sophisticated now!'

'Does that apply to me too?'

'Of course. If you fail playing abroad I don't think people back home think any less of you. They just blame your Spanish or Italian clubs for messing you about!'

Darren still couldn't find a crack in the armour. He was running out of argument. 'But, boss, this could be brilliant for us if we work at it! When I got that first goal the other night, the hairs on the back of my neck stood up at the noise! That's the first time that's ever happened. Because it *is* a new experience here!'

Dawes was wearying of all this now. It was time to get personal.

'So how come you brought your missus with you then?'

Darren was surprised by this tack. 'I guess because I hope she can share in this . . .' he improvised.

Dawes smirked. 'Bollocks – you were frightened! Clinging to what you knew for security!'

Darren was stung by this, because it was to a large extent true. He couldn't stop himself retaliating in kind. 'I suppose I just wanted to avoid having to pay for it!'

Darren wasn't prepared for the ferocity of Dawes's response, but then he didn't know how much Michael Hurley had wounded Dawes. Now the manager was cocking his right fist and grabbing at Darren's shirt-front.

'I ought to smash your face in for that!' He backed Darren up against a tree-trunk. 'Now listen! You go your way, and I'll go mine. And you stay the player and I'll stay the boss. That way, we'll get along fine!'

Dawes released his grip and stalked angrily back towards the hotel. Darren hung his head and ran his fingers through his hair in despair. Then he retreated

130

to his hotel room to confess defeat to Vila, who was lying on his bed, flicking through a pin-up magazine.

'Not only did I *not* persuade Dawes to change his mind, I end up talking myself into his black book.'

'Don't let him get to you, Stanley. And don't let the captain manipulate you again. Leave it to me . . . I will stir the shit, yes?'

Darren had to smile at Vila's grasp of key English phrases. '*You?* You should have stopped me!' he said, in mock indignation.

Vila didn't pick up on the irony. 'I'm not your nanny! Besides, I did my bit. I told the President about Dawes's plans for the pitch . . .'

This was a stunner. '*You* did?'

'Sure, I ring him up with the strange voice . . .' Vila distorted his voice by dropping it at least two octaves. '*Buenos dias, Senor Presidente* . . .'

Darren shook his head in amusement. Now Vila affected seriousness. 'You think I want to spend my time kicking long balls to the corners of the pitch? A groin-strain for me is a disaster, because then I cannot . . .' Vila pumped the air with his forearm.

'All right, I get the picture . . . I didn't realise you were such a purist.'

Vila sat up and swung his legs off the bed.

'Listen, Stanley – this is the truth. If Utrillo or some-body else wants to stop Dawes, you let them do it. Fight your own battles not other people's. We may be a team, but we all have to win on our own.'

Darren registered the message. He would have to find another way to break down Dawes.

By now, back in Barcelona, Senora Torbado's party was under way. Claire arrived to find a thoroughly sophisticated spectacle before her. She'd put on one of her own jacket-and-trouser combinations, thinking smart but casual, but here was a tuxedo-wearing pianist playing lightly, and overdressed guests sampling an up-market finger buffet served by black-tied waiters, while their colleagues served wine and champagne.

Claire could feel herself retreating into her shell. She wasn't fluent enough in Spanish yet to strike up a conversation. And she couldn't see Senora Torbado, the only person she could cling to for company and introductions. After taking a drink, she edged to the side of the main room, and found herself studying the bookshelves.

Fortunately, Senora Torbado soon emerged from a group in the garden, leading a tall, tanned man in his mid-thirties across to Claire. She was gushingly grateful for the attention.

'I told you I'd find him for you, Claire.' She turned to the man on her arm. 'Rafael – you must meet my new friend Claire Travis. Rafael Jiminez.'

Claire and Rafael shook hands. Claire could hardly believe she'd touched him. One of Europe's top fashion designers of the 1980s, Jiminez had shops in the best cities of the world, but kept his core studio in his native Barcelona. Senora Torbado hovered with diplomatic ease in order to get the conversation going.

'I've seen some of your work in London,' Claire ventured. 'I loved it.'

'Thank you,' Rafael said with a smile which revealed dazzlingly white teeth.

'Now look, Claire,' Senora Torbado said briskly, 'Barcelona isn't a city where one hides one's candle if one designs. English reserve will not do. Tell Rafael all about yourself.'

Claire shrugged. 'I do some fashion stuff myself.'

Senora Torbado admonished her immediately. '*Claire!* I've seen her portfolio, Rafael, and it's marvellous.'

'I wouldn't go that far . . .' Claire muttered, feeling

she was being dropped in the deep end. Senora Torbado pitched on regardless. 'And the other thing you should know about Claire is that she's engaged to this young footballer, Darren Matthews of Barca!'

Rafael not only seemed to know the name, but was also obviously impressed.

'Yes, I've seen him play. He could be great. He is not like most English players. He has imagination.'

'If the coach lets him use it,' Claire volunteered.

Rafael was onto it in a flash. 'Tell me, tell me!'

Claire took a deep breath. This wasn't what she imagined she'd be talking about. 'Well, it's like this . . .'

It emerged that Rafael, in between travelling the globe with his designs, always set time aside for the first love of his life – F.C. Barcelona. Claire could hardly ignore this gift and soon found herself dangling the bait of a meeting with Darren before Rafael. She almost but not quite hated herself for using Darren in this way. Besides, Rafael was just as keen to make much of this contact.

As she left the party, Claire found herself hailed by him and given his business card.

'Give me a ring some time – bring your designs in.'

Claire looked embarrassed. 'Look, I wasn't out to hustle you. Senora Torbado just . . .'

'I know what she's like. It's okay. Bring Darren if he wishes. I have some things I think he would like.'

For an instant Claire wondered who was doing the hustling. 'I think he's just signed a new clothing contract actually,' she said defensively.

Rafael seemed not at all put out. 'See you again.'

He wandered away to be enveloped in the arms of a tall, elegant woman, who looked an obvious fashion model. Claire watched and wondered. It was a clear business opportunity. She just wished that Rafael had been more interested in her than in Darren.

Barca's match with Osasuna proved to be a desperate affair. The team played with complete caution, packing the midfield and risking nothing. Midway through the second half, another long-ball pass, this time from Wim Cuipers, set up Darren for a run on goal, which he was able to tuck away low past the home goalkeeper. Darren was pleased enough, but Dawes quickly issued instructions to close the game down with twenty minutes left.

This gave fuel to the moaners on the long coach trip back to Barcelona. Petersen and Cuipers argued about the merits of the performance.

'We kill the game now, not the opposition!' Petersen declared. Darren was exhausted by the in-fighting. He was doing okay. Maybe Vila was right. He should let someone else fight the battle from now on. Tiredness ambushed him, and he fell asleep, head lolling against the window as the coach sped through the intense darkness of the Spanish mountains.

By the time he got home, Darren had found a new spin on his attitude to life in Barcelona. He was too pliable, too willing to play the role other people expected of him. He would have to find his own voice and be prepared to use it. The first opportunity arrived when he went off with Nick for the fashion photo-shoot which had been arranged as part of Darren's deal with the chain-store.

To his dismay, he found himself up in the scrubby woodlands high above the city, modelling clothes which were an exact copy of the English country-squire look, complete with twelve-bore shotgun and shooting-bag.

'If I'd known this was the deal I'd have got Kenny Dawes to take my place,' he complained to Nick. 'This isn't what I'm about, Nick. I'd never wear this gear in real life. I'm peddling English stereotypes to the Spanish!'

Nick wagged a warning finger. 'Don't knock it! What would you get in England? You and Vinny Jones modelling for Millet's?'

Nevertheless, Darren forced Nick to re-negotiate the contract, allowing Darren to choose the type of clothes he thought suited him.

There was one other matter he needed to sort out. Eva. Darren had worked out that despite the lush fantasy of their afternoon together, he was probably being treated as no more than a bangle for one of her designer bracelets – footballer, writer, actor and whoever else a bored rich girl could get her hands on. He thought it best to confront her directly, and drove over to her apartment after training the following week.

His suspicions were confirmed almost as soon as he parked his car. There she was, leaving the block with a pony-tailed dandy on her arm. She saw Darren, she definitely saw him, and then looked away, keeping up a conversation with her companion in Spanish.

'I was just calling by to tell you I can't see you again . . .' he called out. Eva kept walking without so much as a backward glance. Darren smiled, he felt unburdened suddenly, on his way to self-discovery. He mimed a powerful volley with his right foot and imagined the ball smashing high into the net . . .

Chapter Seven

Claire duly took up Rafael Jiminez's invitation to take her work round to his studio. She'd told Darren about it, and he'd been surprisingly positive, when she'd expected a cautious, perhaps even suspicious reaction. She guessed that Darren had been flattered by Rafael's endorsement of his footballing talent. At a certain level of the game – and playing for Barcelona was definitely up there – footballers became the wish-fulfilment objects of contemporaries who were successful in other areas. Rock stars who'd always wanted to play for their local team invited footballers backstage. Similarly, designers, restaurateurs, actors, and stand-up comedians would be delighted to have a player hobnobbing with them.

Claire had always thought it was also to do with the fact that footballers somehow hung on to their street credibility longer because, by definition, they had to stay with their public. She also thought, a little slyly, that the arty types desperately needed to prove to themselves that they were in 'manly' professions, and a footballer's presence in their social circle provided testimony. For the footballer, the attraction was simple – a recognition that he was up there with the big-earners, with the cultural icons, of the day.

So as she made her way through the warren of alleys in the Barrio Gotic, trying to locate Rafael's shop and

studio, she felt very much that she was really an emiss-
ary from Darren to Rafael, preparing the day for when
the two men met and basked in the glow of each other's
success.

The shop, styled simply 'Jiminez', proved to be strategically placed, just a couple of turns away from the
famous Picasso Museum. Rafael therefore had easy
access to that most valuable of communities, the Japan-
ese tourist. There were a handful in the shop as Claire
was escorted through to the back and then up a narrow
staircase to the upper floors.

Here, the rooms had been opened out and illuminated by skylights and huge windows. Rafael had two
floors of white-painted, airy, studio space, and a huge
penthouse as his living area – it was 'loft' living, Barcelona style.

He reacted pleasantly to Claire's arrival, remembering her name effortlessly, and kissing her cheek.
Then for the next forty minutes – God, what would this
cost at his going rate, wondered Claire! – Rafael studied
the designs she'd done since her arrival in Barcelona,
and all the other fragments she had been confident
enough to include in her portfolio. Rafael spread the
sheets of drawings out onto a large plan-chest and
reacted quickly.

'Great shapes . . . nice clean lines . . . the colours
are fantastic,' he purred.

'Thank you. I guess I've been thinking differently
now I'm in a sunny country. The trouble with England
is that you find yourself only using browns, greens and
greys!'

Rafael made one more run through the pages. 'I like
these a lot, Claire. You have a really good eye. These
are an excellent start, but I'm sure you can do better.'

He started to fold up the drawings. Claire felt
instantly deflated. That was it? 'A so-far-so-good' crit,

138

now piss off! And then almost abstractly through her disappointment, she heard Rafael say, 'Okay, I will commission, what? – five, maybe six designs from you?'

'Commission?' Claire could barely get the word out. 'I don't know what to say . . .'

Rafael smiled at her nervousness. 'You say, "Yes, Rafael, I would love to have lunch with you now!"'

He walked her expertly through the Barrio Gotic, giving her notes on the little food shops or hidden cafés that were his favourites in this corner of the city which seemed almost shut off from the world. They emerged by the cathedral square, a brief interlude of daylight, before he escorted her into the unobtrusive doorway of a restaurant called 'La Odisea'. Her journey now felt like an odyssey – from art college, to bumming around Paris, to renting a shop in a provincial town. Suddenly here she was in Barcelona, in a restaurant that seemed part private club, part art gallery, having lunch with one of the best designers in the world. Claire had to keep pinching her hand to convince herself that she was awake.

Throughout the next few weeks, Claire worked frantically, but enjoyably, in the room at the house which she'd turned into a studio. Darren appeared to be very supportive, despite the fact that all he saw of her some days was the back of her head, hunched over a drawing board. He'd changed, thought Claire – matured. Only occasionally did the nagging suspicion recur that Darren was only 'allowing' this so he could cosy up to Jiminez.

As he left the house one Monday morning, dressed in club blazer, en route to the away leg of a first-round European Cup tie in Albania, Darren tossed the keys of the Merc to Claire.

'Impress your designer friend,' he said, knowing that Claire was due to have lunch with him. Claire was puzzled. Rafael had already seen her in the car at Senora Torbado's party.

'I'd rather my work impressed him than your Mercedes.'

'Every little helps. I want him to take you seriously.'

'That's kind,' Claire muttered, still unsure of Darren's motives. She guessed that he might be 'showing-off' to Jiminez, just letting him know that he, Darren, had a few bob too. But then, Rafael already seemed in awe of Darren – what difference could a car make?

Darren loaded his case into the back of the waiting taxi and curled his arms round Claire's waist.

'I just want you to know you're very precious to me.'

They kissed. Darren seemed distracted. He couldn't be worrying about flying. The game would be a walk-over. Okay, Albania had pockets of unrest, but it wasn't Bosnia. And then it hit Claire – the unmistakable truth as to why Darren was behaving like this. He was jealous!

'Hope the lunch goes well . . .' said Darren getting into the taxi.

Claire watched as it pulled away from the house. Now she could see things from his point of view. She had a lunch date with a rich designer, and two whole days and nights on her own. He'd put two and two together and got sixty-nine. Silly boy. Claire waltzed back into the house and returned to her work.

At Nou Camp the players gathered and watched as the coach taking them to the airport was loaded up with skips and all manner of containers. For a trip like this, into 'rough terrain', nothing was left to chance. They took their own food and borrowed two chefs from a five-star hotel to travel with them and cook it. They took their own bottled water. They had medicines of all kind, and also doctors and physiotherapists to accompany them. It was, Darren reflected, a little like preparing for war.

The players and Dawes, supervised by Vice-President Gamez, soon boarded. Vaqueras was missing out on this trip – lucky man – and Gamez was plainly taking it as a test of his organisational powers. He twittered and fluttered, quite out of character. Dawes wondered how much of a pest he'd be on the trip.

The coach drove straight on to the tarmac at Barcelona Airport and parked alongside the Iberia jet which the club had chartered. The spare spaces were sold off to the travelling press pack, who waited in their own coach. Nearly a hundred people would be travelling, just for one tiny match in a backwater of Europe.

Dawes had a quiet moan to Darren. 'If it'd been up to me, I'd have had us fly out the morning of the game, eat on the plane, change on the coach and fly out as soon as it was over!'

Darren took this as a momentary thaw in their now frosty relationship. But he also knew that a squad of players, cooped up in a hotel for forty-eight hours, and tense before a game, would be getting on each other's nerves very soon.

The flight to Tirana, the capital of Albania, took less than ninety minutes, but as they landed, the players, peering out at this still mysterious country, must have thought they'd passed through a time warp.

Standing on the tarmac to greet them was a brass band straight out of Ruritania, all feathered hats and bum notes, flanked by a formal reception committee of diplomats. There was even a red carpet.

Darren followed Vila out onto the steps from the aircraft, surveying the near comical scene. Vila saw nothing at all humorous.

'Stanley, the next two days will be the longest of your life!'

'They seem friendly enough.'

'That is not for us! They will all be hoping to hi-jack the plane to escape!'

As they reached the bottom of the steps, both were kissed on the cheek by a diplomat with a moustache like a yard-brush.

Claire's lunch was an altogether more sophisticated affair. Rafael had picked 'El Tragaluz', a three-storey restaurant in a shopping mall, just off the top of the Ramblas. A café was topped by a brasserie, which in turn had a more formal restaurant above it. Here on this floor, the roof had been stripped out and replaced by glass panels, hung with wooden Venetian blinds. The walls had an earthy, brick-like roughness, but the large cushioned chairs and the starched white napery were comfort itself.

The room was quite full and Claire noticed that heads were turning as she joined Rafael at his table. It was obviously a place at which the arty and the trendy liked to be seen. Rafael stood to kiss her. A bottle of white wine in a cooler was already on the table, and he quickly poured her a glass. Claire complimented him on his choice of restaurant. Rafael knew the owner, of course, and the designer. A good job she liked it, thought Claire.

Rafael suggested a few dishes to try, and soon they ordered. He sat back in his chair, very much at home in this environment where fashion, food, design and celebrity were the elements blended together.

'So how are you getting on with the work?' he asked, not pointedly but casually.

'Okay. I'm a little nervous, you understand?'

'No need. You have a fantastic eye.'

Rafael suddenly reached across and touched the dress that Claire was wearing close to her neck.

'This is one of yours, I presume?'

Claire shrugged, bashful at being caught out so soon. 'Well, if you've made it, flaunt it, as my old tutor used to say!'

'But don't rush; when you feel ready for me to see them, *that* will be the time to get nervous!'

He now patted Claire's hand. Claire couldn't help noticing that the level of physical contact was increasing. Fortunately, the moment was broken by the arrival at the table of a tall model, dressed dramatically all in black. Rafael stood immediately and the model slid her pencil-thin body into his hands. Their conversation was hushed, intimate and, to complete Claire's exclusion, conducted in Catalan.

Claire fiddled self-consciously with her wine-glass, awaiting an introduction. It didn't come. The model broke free and left without a second glance at Claire. Rafael resumed his seat.

'Camilla's one of my regular models. You remember her from *Vogue*?'

'Sorry to say this, but they all look the same to me. Like a pile of wire coat-hangers in a plastic bag.'

Rafael laughed out loud. 'Because, of course, you're looking at the clothes rather than the body?'

'That *is* what the business is about, isn't it?'

Rafael hunched his shoulders in disagreement. 'Not only. I always tell myself that I am creating fantasies for the women who buy my clothes.' Claire became aware that his dark brown Spanish eyes were trying to lock themselves onto her. 'I want a woman to feel . . . transformed when she wears one of my designs. Freed, to do as she wishes.'

'Maybe you should print that on the washing advice label?'

Rafael smiled, realising that Claire wasn't buying this nonsense.

'Quite right, Claire. I'm too serious.' He sipped his wine.

Claire felt suspiciously as if she had scored a little victory over him. All the mystical syrup and the heavy eye-contact looked and sounded like his Grade 1 chat-up routine. The fact that it hadn't worked on her had plainly unsettled him. So Claire now had to deal with the possibility that all Rafael's words of encouragement were merely stages of an intended conquest. If that was the case, the question became one of how far he was prepared to go to get her, and how far she was prepared to let him.

After lunch, Rafael insisted on taking Claire across to the Parc Joan Miró, an open space dedicated to one of Catalonia's most famous designers, sculptors and painters. In the centre of the park, at the heart of an ornamental pond, stood one of Miró's most dramatic sculptures: 'Woman and Bird'. Claire tried hard to ignore any symbolic significance as Rafael suddenly began to talk to her, in Spanish, about her engagement to Darren.

'*Cuando esta su matrimonio, Claire?*'

Claire was flustered. 'Sorry, Rafael, I haven't got the vocabulary to deal with this yet.'

Rafael took a pull on his fat Cuban cigar and blew smoke-rings up into the air. 'It's okay, tell me in English why you are not married yet.'

Claire wondered why this had suddenly got personal. She could hardly avoid the question, but she managed to fashion a limited answer.

'Lots of reasons. We haven't lived together much. We also wanted to see how we got on in Spain.'

'Travel can put a strain on a relationship. My marriage broke up when we lived in Japan. My wife

144

was homesick. I was working twenty hours a day.'

Claire relaxed suddenly, trading confidences was at least a two-way street. 'I didn't know you'd been married.'

Rafael gave her a wistful smile. 'It was five years ago. The scars aren't always visible.'

Claire couldn't square this sense of regret with her images of him curling his arms around nubile fashion models.

'You don't seem short of female company.'

'No, but sometimes I wish I had just one person in my life. Which is why I envy you and Darren.'

'We've had our struggles . . . but we're steadier now. Coming abroad has helped. We've had to lean on each other a little more.'

'That's good.'

Claire had misjudged him. This wasn't the pushy, smarmy individual she'd seen in operation at the restaurant. Maybe her sarcasm had been enough to rebuff him. Then suddenly he said, 'Does Darren feel threatened by me?'

Claire frowned. This was mischievous. 'Why should he?' she threw back at him.

'Well, I'm here with you, and he's away with the team.'

Claire felt she'd heard enough evidence for a prosecution now. 'Look, I'm trying hard to make my relationship with Darren work. This doesn't help, Rafael.'

'If this is bothering you, then maybe you're unsure of your feelings.'

Claire's face tightened. 'Is that part of our deal then; my designs only get used if I go to bed with you?'

Now Rafael frowned. He backed away from her. 'Claire, please, I don't operate this way. With models, yes. It's the currency of the fashion business. But I can

145

tell you how much I like you, can't I? There's no harm in this, is there?'

'You tell me. Part of me thinks you're only interested in my work because I live with a Barca footballer.'

Rafael smiled broadly. 'Now that *would* be perverted. I just think that you are talented and beautiful . . . and sensitive.'

He was putting a marker down. Letting her know his feelings so that she would have to take the initiative. Or would at least be less surprised if he did. Claire couldn't help but be flattered by his attention though.

'So, you know how I feel.' He smiled. 'In the meantime, we're in business together.'

They reached the exit to the park. Rafael hailed a taxi for Claire and they went their separate ways.

The team's hotel in central Tirana was an archaic and slightly run-down affair, with lots of wood-panelling and old furniture. It was probably an old Communist Party haunt. But it was still the best that Tirana could offer in the circumstances. The streets of the city had been dotted with ox-carts and horse-drawn trucks as the coach had brought the team in from the airport. So nobody was expecting much by the time they saw the hotel.

After they'd taken their bags to their rooms, the players gathered at Dawes's and Gamez's request in the lobby for what they thought would be a briefing on their schedule for the two and a bit days till the match against Dinamo Tirana. Gamez offered translations for those who couldn't understand Dawes – and they would be in the majority.

'I want you to get a couple of hours' rest now,' he began, 'and then we'll do a bit of light training later this afternoon.'

The players nodded their approval; this seemed

reasonable. But Dawes had other points to make.

'Apart from that, you know the rules on a trip like this: one, only drink bottled water; two, only eat stuff that our chefs have prepared; three, no sight-seeing or tourist crap. There's sod-all to see anyway, and the locals can't be trusted. This is strictly business!'

Utrillo's hand shot up. He hadn't liked this patronising and insulting dismissal of the host country. He muttered in Spanish.

'What's he saying, Roberto?' Dawes asked of Gamez.

'He wants to point out that Albania is now a democracy and that we should show our goodwill to the people.'

Dawes smirked. 'Show goodwill? I think the club doctor will have something to say about that. Your goodwill stays in your trousers!'

Utrillo didn't need a translation. He reacted with distaste.

Dawes's gaze fell upon Vila. 'Anyone breaking these rules will be fined – *heavily*. Understand, Senor Vila?'

Vila affected complete innocence. The meeting broke up, with most of the players heading for their rooms for a nap.

Gamez, though, had sensed the captain's irritation at Dawes's ill-advised tirade against Tirana. Knowing that Utrillo could cause trouble if angered and thereby blight the trip and Gamez's management, he wanted to prevent any further tension.

'I don't think the country is as backward as you make it out to be,' Gamez protested.

'These players are from Mars as far as the people here are concerned! They're glamorous! Exotic! Now, if the locals see money to be made or the chance to shag their way into Western Europe, they're gonna take it. And I don't want my players messed about before a game!'

This seemed as much a warning to Gamez as it did to the players. Dawes stalked off to organise sentry duty.

Darren had stretched out on the over-firm single-bed in the hotel room, and was about to drift off when he felt his nose being tickled. He opened his eyes. A fistful of $50 bills were being wafted under his nose. His room-mate was standing over him.

'These are our passports to a good time, Stanley.'

'Eh?' asked Darren, clearing his head. 'What, *here*?'

'*Si, si – el dolar es el rey del mundo!*' Vila exclaimed, getting all excited.

'It's the king of nothing when the manager bans us from leaving the hotel!'

'Sorry to say, Stanley – but your compatriot is an idiot. He messes with the team's tactics, now he tries to stop me achieving my ambition.'

Darren frowned. 'Winning the away leg of a European Cup tie in Albania?'

Vila swatted Darren across the face with the dollars. 'Como, Stanley! Wake up! In every country I have played a game of football, I have . . . *que es el expresion Americano? Ah, si!* "Hidden the salami!" yes?'

Darren reacted wearily. It was like having a dog on heat in the room. 'Yes, yes, and you don't want to miss out on whatever Albania has to offer?'

Vila waved the dollars with a cheeky grin on his face. 'With these, no problem!'

Darren sat up on the bed. '"Around the World in 80 Lays" – be a good title for your autobiography.' Vila tucked the money away inside his jacket.

'So tonight we . . .'

Darren held up his hand, interrupting him before he got any further. He knew what was coming. 'Sorry, count me out. I'm trying to leave all that stuff behind me now.'

Vila darkened. Could this be the same Darren who'd found a *pija* so enticing. 'No more fun with the rich girls?'

'Wasn't much to be had anyway. Besides, I've decided I like being faithful. Makes life less complicated.'

Vila suddenly looked solemn; he sat on his bed across the narrow room from Darren. 'You think I am a caveman, yes?'

'Certainly snore like one,' Darren joked, sensing Vila's sudden change of mood.

'Let me tell you something. I married when I was eighteen. I was a virgin. Still working in a factory. Playing football was just for fun. Then I am signed by Barca for their junior team. Suddenly my world opens up!'

'It does for all of us who make it,' Darren said blandly, wondering what Vila's point might be. Now Vila hung his head, avoiding Darren's look.

'Nobody in the squad knows this . . . I trust you not to tell them. I cannot have children. I am a gun with no bullets.' Vila looked up. Darren could tell this was no joke.

'I'm sorry . . . I'm really sorry.'

'God has played a joke on me, huh? So I will never be able to play football in the garden with my sons.'

'What about adoption?'

'Maybe. When I have finished playing. But for now, I am still angry with God. I also know that soon I will be a sad old man, with legs like a donkey. So because I am a footballer, I can live the life that ordinary men only dream about. That's what I tell myself.'

Darren shrugged. 'If it makes you happy . . .'

Vila laughed ruefully. 'Maybe, maybe not. Playing the clown is only good when people are laughing.' Vila

149

stood up. 'I have talked too much.' He crossed to the window, and opened the doors onto the balcony.

'What are you doing?' asked Darren suspiciously.

'Dawes has *three* men in the lobby, making sure I do not escape!' Now Vila swung a leg over the end of the balcony. 'Romeo has found his ladder! *Buenos tardes*, Stanley!'

With that, Vila disappeared from view. Darren didn't want to think what he would be up to. He closed his eyes and lay back on the bed, hoping time would pass quicker that way.

Claire had retired to bed. Drinking at lunchtime usually deadened her for the rest of the day, so she'd settled on an early night, catching up with some of the Spanish fashion magazines and waiting for Darren to phone from Albania, technology permitting. She was about to put the lights off when the phone next to the bed rang. 'Finally found an Albanian phone-box,' she muttered as she stretched across to pick up the receiver. There was a hissing noise and other interference. She banged the phone to try and clear it . . . 'Darren? Darren, is that you?'

But the interference wasn't Albanian in source. The call was coming from Rafael's car-phone, which Claire quickly realised when the line suddenly cleared. The sound of traffic noise mingled in the background with jazz music. It transpired that Rafael just happened to be driving up to the Merbeye Bar where a jazz quartet was playing. The bar stayed open till 3 a.m. It was only 11 p.m. The night was young. Could he entice her out for a night-cap? . . . and several other lines from American movies came down the line. He even went to the extent of holding out the phone to pick up the sound of the quartet playing.

Claire turned over on her stomach, amused by

150

Rafael's prompting. 'Look, why don't you just hold out the phone for an hour and that will save me having to travel . . .'

Rafael bantered some more; it was all light-weight and fun, and then he made one last invite and hung up. Claire thought about it – 11 p.m. was pretty early by Barcelona standards. It would only take ten minutes to get up to the bar. And now she felt reasonably refreshed after her lie-down . . . these were the spurious points stacking up on the 'yes' pile. Darren hadn't phoned, or hadn't been able to get through, and was unlikely to call now. She thought she'd risk an hour out, and see more of Rafael in action. After all, it was the only way to find out precisely what she felt about him.

Presumptuous was one of the words to formulate in Claire's mind about Rafael. As at lunchtime, he'd already decided what she should be drinking – tonight there were Brandy Alexanders on the table as she arrived. Still, could have been worse. She'd lost count of the tedious guys in cocktail bars over the years who'd asked her if she'd wanted a 'slow comfortable screw'. And Rafael was at least prepared to explain his passion for jazz without assuming that she shared it.

'The best music comes from pain, that's what makes jazz great!'

Claire sipped the first layer of cream, flecked with chocolate. 'I'm afraid I don't buy the "suffering artist" view of life.'

Rafael looked put out. 'Well, my best work came after my marriage was wrecked. It was how I pulled myself up again. You don't believe that we gain from these times in our lives?'

Claire shook her head. 'Too many of the people at my college used *angst* as a disguise for not having any talent. I guess I just believe in the virtues of hard work.'

151

'My God, very Protestant! This explains why Darren attracts you.'

'What's that supposed to mean?' Claire asked sharply.

'Well, he is beginning to put hard work before his skill.'

'Only because the manager forces him to be like that.'

Rafael persisted with his attack. 'The papers are already asking if he is still too English and not enough Spanish . . .'

Two more Brandy Alexanders were delivered. He must have ordered them in bulk, Claire thought as she shifted in her chair so that she could face him. 'Look, I don't find slagging off Darren too entertaining. I admire the way he's been able to improve himself. He was going nowhere until a few years ago.'

'But tell me, Claire. Has Darren *suffered*?'

Claire dug her heels in. 'I'm sorry, I don't see the connection.'

Rafael started the next drink. 'Take George Best. Or Maradona. Poor backgrounds. Lots of problems. But great players.'

Claire was on shaky ground here, but she wasn't going to give in to this argument. 'Yes, but . . . they inflicted the suffering upon themselves. Their greatness didn't come *out* of it, did it?'

Rafael wagged a finger at her. 'But these flaws made them more than just footballers! By letting go, they found their spirit, their creativity!'

'Look, self-indulgence doesn't go down too well in England. If you get called a "flair" player, you're as good as dead.' Claire took a great slug of her drink hoping Rafael would change tack. He did, but only as he moved himself closer to her.

'All right, I prefer to call it self-expression. You and I both know what it was like to be at art school. We were encouraged to express ourselves. To create chaos. And then find sense and direction.'

This seemed more plausible to Claire, but then art wasn't football as far as she was concerned. And she was damned if she was going to lose this argument. She tried to deflect him with a joke.

'Well, at my college it was more a case of finding your way home after five bottles of barley wine.'

Rafael matched it again. 'Ah, yes, I drank these once in London. After three, I was in Trafalgar Square and Nelson's Column was swaying.'

Claire smiled at the memory, and with relief that the heaviness had lifted from the conversation.

'I would just like Darren to enjoy the same pleasure of self-expression that you and I know!' Rafael said reasonably.

'Well maybe he can,' Claire said defiantly as the quartet finished a set to loud applause. The waiter arrived with two more drinks. Claire finished her second and felt a pleasant wooziness creep over her. It was art school all over again.

She woke up the next morning staring at a bright white ceiling. After blinking several times, she established that she still had control of her vital movements, although any tilt of the head produced a vague throb. Her mouth felt like a small rodent had spent the night in it. Gradually she looked around to realise the worst – she was in Rafael's penthouse. She tried to rewind the video-tape in her mind, but the picture was fuzzy. She could now hear a knocking. Claire sat up a little; there at the bedroom door was a fully clothed Rafael, carrying a breakfast tray.

'May I come in?' he asked.

153

'Sure . . .' Claire said, not certain that she meant it. 'Sorry about this.'

Rafael slid the tray onto the bed in front of her. 'You were only sick between the car and the house – very disciplined.'

Claire winced. The picture had just come back. 'What a mess! Sorry.'

'Stop apologising!' Rafael ordered. 'It was me who made you come out drinking!'

'Me who accepted,' Claire muttered, chastising herself. She took a sip of fruit juice from the tray on which there was coffee, and croissants and jam.

'Thank you, Rafael,' she said sheepishly.

'For what?'

'Well, you know . . .'

'That's okay. It would have been mad for you to drive.'

'I meant for . . . God, how can I *use* this phrase? For not taking advantage of me.'

Rafael frowned. 'I've never heard this expression before. Must be very English . . .'

'Uniquely I'd say. It's to do with the idea that a lot of English men have, that they must get a woman drunk before she's willing to have sex with them.'

Rafael shook his head in bewilderment. 'This is crazy. If a man thinks like that, he must have as bad an opinion of himself as he does of women.' Rafael patted Claire's hand. 'You were terrific, by the way – a wild animal. You don't remember?'

Claire smiled at him, pleased that he could see the funny side of what must have been a pretty disastrous evening for him.

'I'd better be getting home. I have work to do for you . . .'

Rafael crossed the room and opened a heavy wooden door to reveal a hi-tech bathroom, glistening with stainless steel units and radiators. 'All yours,' he said, leaving Claire to her breakfast.

The Barca team had negotiated, as a traditional courtesy, one training session on the pitch of Dinamo Tirana's stadium. Dawes led the players down a dark, peeling tunnel and out across a shale running track onto the pitch. Even a cursory glance revealed that there were a large number of bumps across the full width of the pitch and that it was pock-marked with tufts of grass.

'Bleeding cabbage patch!' Dawes exploded. He began to empty a netting bag of training balls, which he proceeded to boot out all over the pitch in disgust. The players, unmoved by his tirade, began their warm-up exercises and stretches. Darren caught Dawes's eye as he stood hands on hips surveying the wasteland around him.

'We'll need a good first touch on this, eh boss!' Darren said conversationally, hoping to cheer Dawes up.

'Like hell!' Dawes scoffed. 'That's just what they'll want, us poncing around on the ball. No, this battle will be strictly aerial, son! I should take a Panadol for your headache now!'

Darren got the picture instantly – a tight formation, him chasing a long ball, or trying to get on the end of set-piece kicks. It was a desultory prospect; the people here deserved to see their rich, exalted visitors turn on a bit of style, surely?

But Dawes was already set on his pattern for the match. The training exercises revealed more of what passed for his thinking. Darren was stationed alone in one goalmouth, while Petersen and Cuipers fed him high crosses from either wing. Vila took up a fairly token presence in goal, and was soon winding Darren up.

155

'I have seen fleas jump higher than you, Stanley . . .'

Darren thumped a header past him in retaliation. 'In whatever bed you slept in last night, probably.'

Vila smirked at him. 'I was too busy to sleep!'

Another cross came bulleting in from the wing, Darren jumped but got his timing wrong and the ball skidded off the top of his head and plopped harmlessly into Vila's arms.

'Kinnell, Stanley! And this is with no defenders! We have no chance of scoring tomorrow!'

'Well, let's hope not . . . it may change our coach's mind about his cowardly tactics.'

Darren missed the next cross completely, and took a breather, hands resting on his knees.

After an hour, Dawes brought an end to the proceedings and ushered his players back towards the coach waiting right by the stadium entrance. With their training gear muddied and sweat-stained, the players looked anything but appealing. Nevertheless a sizeable crowd of local youngsters hung around looking for autographs or free gifts. Dawes barked at his players, urging them back on the coach. He darkened visibly when he saw Utrillo scribbling away among a group of teenagers, chatting to the oldest member of the group.

'Oi, *capitano*! On the bus, *por favor*!'

Utrillo turned and glowered at Dawes, continuing to listen as the young man talked.

'*Un momento, por favor* . . .'

'*Now!*' Dawes screamed. 'Or you can kiss goodbye to the armband!' Utrillo muttered a last few words to the young man before breaking away. He ignored Dawes completely as he stepped back onto the bus.

In the seclusion of the hotel, the players sat about resting, trying to blank their minds of any form of entertainment. In the lobby Dawes held a brief press conference for the travelling sports journalists, some of whom had been at the training session, and had therefore guessed at a defensive formation. Not that Dawes would confirm it. The press also wanted to know if the players were getting bored being stuck in the hotel.

'I hope so,' Dawes said gleefully, 'because then the match will come as a welcome relief for them!'

Jordi Bassas, one of the younger, more radical generation of Catalan sports journalists, but a noted scruffbag, held up his hand earnestly. 'Do you regard this match as easy?'

Dawes could see a trap of sorts, but wasn't going to jump into it. 'Absolutely not,' he said emphatically. 'European competition is vital to the wealth of the club. And if you don't win *here* then the glamour of the final stages will be irrelevant. This is a match we have to take very seriously. So there's a bottle of champagne reward for any of you who spot a Barca player on the streets.'

Bassas laughed, then stopped when he realised that Dawes wasn't joking. Over lunch a certain spirit of mutiny began to grow among the squad. They resented being treated as hostages by the manager. The diningroom, with its dark brown paint and fading portrait of King Zog of Albania, certainly did little to lift their spirits. The 'Gang of Four' – Vila, Cuipers, Petersen and Darren – sat at one end of the long table, swapping assorted moans.

'So this afternoon – no movies. No cabaret shows to go to. No exciting restaurants. No girls to meet. And still twenty-six hours and forty-one minutes till the match,' Cuipers said mournfully.

Vila offered him his fruit knife, handle first, and mimed a wrist-slashing gesture.

'Maybe we could find some animals, and race them – have a few bets,' suggested Petersen.

'Plenty of rats in the kitchen for sure,' said Vila.

157

Darren was just wondering why he still couldn't get any answer from Claire on the phone.

Into this long-faced bunch strolled Utrillo, who put his hand on Darren's shoulders.

'Darren, *un momento, por favor*.'

Darren was almost grateful for the interruption. '*Si, naturalmente, Manuel!*'

Utrillo beckoned Darren out of the room. Vila, the polar opposite of the politically aware Utrillo, couldn't resist a dig. 'Hey, comrade,' he called out to Utrillo, gesturing all around him. 'What do you think of what forty years of Communism gave this country?'

Utrillo refused to rise to the bait. 'They had *Stalinism* not Communism,' he corrected, as he opened the dining-room door for Darren. They moved out into the corridor and crossed into the lobby, seating themselves away from any club officials.

'Darren, I need your help,' said Utrillo gravely.

'If it involves complaining to Dawes again, leave me out of it.'

'This is more important. The young man I was speaking with at the stadium. It is he who needs our help. He is a social worker . . . he is in charge of an orphanage. They have no money, no medicine . . .'

'So – it's their government's problem, isn't it? Nothing *we* can do.' Darren stood to leave. Utrillo pulled him down by his arm. Darren reacted sharply. 'Look, I'm sorry, Manuel, there must be thousands of deserving cases in this country. Why choose them?'

'Because they asked!'

'Yeah, but it's not our job to go round raising money. We're footballers. We entertain. Help people feel better about their lives. That's enough, isn't it?'

'Not any more, Darren. We have the power to change things. Have you not done work for charity in England?'

Darren felt himself getting sucked into the argument. He often sympathised with Utrillo's views, but just wished he wasn't so strident about their relevance.

'Yes, of course. Lost count of the number of signed footballs and shirts I've donated to fund-raising events. And I used to get hundreds of letters a year, all wanting help. But it's not possible to do all the things people want you to do.'

'No, of course not. Darren, may I ask where you learned your football? Right from the start, I mean.'

Darren shrugged. 'Kicking the ball round the garden with my dad.'

'For me, the same. And for every player around the world it will be similar. This is a game which begins in the home. In the family.'

Darren could see his point. 'But there's an awful lot of hard work and risk-taking to get to this level . . .'

'Yes, I know,' said Utrillo. Then he became hushed, almost reverent. 'But what you and I achieve is not because of *merit*! It is because of luck. Chance. That our fathers put a ball at our feet, not a hammer in our hands! That we had fathers at all!'

Darren couldn't help but be touched by this. Ironically, the image that moved him most was the thought of Vila being denied his children.

'Okay, so let's organise a collection from each member of the squad,' Darren suggested.

'They need more than that . . .' Utrillo said, looking around to check they were not being overheard. And then he explained what he thought they should do.

159

Chapter Eight

Had Vila been awake, he would almost certainly have enjoyed the role-reversal of Darren sneaking out of the room in mid-afternoon for a secret assignation. Darren had this as a ready-made alibi in case his room-mate stirred, but the excesses of the previous day had plainly taken their toll on the goalkeeper's constitution. Darren collected a bulky carrier-bag he'd been keeping out of Vila's sight and made his way out of the room.

He slipped down one floor via the fire exit and then entered the hotel kitchens, where two middle-aged Albanians were doing the washing-up. They watched with bemused smiles as Darren opened and then eased his way through the emergency door. After he had gone, one of the washers-up made a sexual semaphore with his right arm and left fist.

Darren scuttled down an alley at the rear of the hotel and, turning a corner onto the street, found Utrillo standing with the journalist Jordi Bassas.

'We're breaking a club curfew, and you bring a journalist along!' Darren said angrily.

Bassas made placatory gestures. 'Darren, it's okay. You can trust me! Manuel told me about the orphanage. I can do a story on this, help pressure the club.'

'The *club*?' Darren asked with a frown. The agenda seemed to have changed since he'd agreed to a secret visit to the orphanage. What was Utrillo up to now?

'I want *them* to put up some money . . .' Before Darren could argue back, Utrillo took him by the arm. 'Come on. Our friend will be waiting.'

Myftar, the orphanage manager, was waiting on the edge of one of Tirana's barren squares, across which carts with two-stroke engines spluttered. He at least had a drab-coloured Skoda to hand. When he saw Utrillo, Darren and Bassas, he beamed with gratitude and opened the rear passenger door for them.

Darren looked out of the window as the car trundled out of the city, passing endless blocks of colourless, low-rise buildings. Here and there, pavements and roads simply became dirt tracks, or large jagged craters which would take an axle off in seconds. Myftar steered the car expertly round these, though occasionally a jaw-shattering bump occurred. Myftar seemed exhilarated by the experience, but then he did have around three million pounds' worth of footballers in his car. He spoke in jagged, broken English.

'You will win match. Five goals to zero. Darren, for you, three goals.'

Darren was still wondering why he'd got into this. Utrillo's initiatives had landed him in trouble before. This one could find him suspended, sacked or maybe even kidnapped if it backfired.

'Our English coach is not so brave as our English centre-forward. How far now, my friend?'

'Three kilometres only.'

Darren winced. His legs were already going to sleep. What if they crashed? Being stiffed in a Skoda would have the obituarists stifling laughter as they wrote.

'We must be back before seven. We have a curfew,' warned Utrillo.

'We had one for forty years!' Myftar shouted over his shoulder, referring to the rule of Enver Hoxha,

Albania's post-war dictator. Somehow, it seemed he might still be alive, as the car drove on through estates of utterly grey, breeze-block dwellings.

Ten minutes later the car pulled to a halt outside a crumbling two-storey building, flanked by rusting iron railings. Myftar opened the doors, and Darren, Utrillo and Bassas squeezed out, rubbing the circulation back into their legs.

Myftar crossed to the gates which fronted the house. They were chained and padlocked. He fetched out a key and released the chain from the gate.

'You keep the children locked in?' Utrillo asked with concern.

'For their safety, yes. Otherwise . . . people steal them, put them to work in factory.'

With the gate opened, they passed through into the courtyard at the rear of the building. Darren had never seen anything like it before. About two dozen boys, aged between nine and fifteen, were milling around in a large room, bare apart from a dozen worn mattresses lying on the floor. The boys wore an ill-assortment of clothes, and they looked thin and undernourished.

As they saw the two footballers arrive, bedlam broke out, with the children excitedly mobbing both Darren and Utrillo. Bassas began to dictate notes onto a pocket recorder, taping the sound of the boys' reaction.

From the carrier-bag he was carrying, Darren now produced one of the squad's old training balls which he had 'acquired' from the team skip. He tossed it to the boys, who grappled for it eagerly. Within seconds, they had begun an impromptu game in the room.

Myftar shouted for silence, and in an instant they all stood to attention. Another command, and they all sat down on the floor. Darren couldn't help noticing the expression of wonder on their faces as they looked at him and Utrillo. Here were two tanned, well-fed, well-clothed men with expensive trinkets on their wrists and around their necks.

'This is room where they must sleep also. I have small kitchen through there. Upstairs one toilet, one shower. This is why we need your help, senors.' Myftar was stooping in what seemed almost a gesture of supplication.

'What happened to their parents?' Darren asked quietly.

Myftar shrugged. 'Some just died. Some, they fled to Italy. Some, killed by the Sigurimi, the old Secret Police.'

'For what?' asked Utrillo anxiously.

'The crime of worshipping a God, when the State said He was not allowed to exist.'

'And now you have freedom, democracy, a market economy,' Utrillo said with heavy irony which was probably lost on Myftar.

'All the things that screw up the Western world,' Bassas added blackly. These comments were no consolation to the children. Utrillo and Darren exchanged looks, moved by the pitiable condition of the boys.

'I ask you to help, because the thing they love most is football,' Myftar said simply.

And now as the evening darkened quickly, Myftar ordered the boys outside. They brought the ball, and within seconds, Utrillo, Bassas and Darren were taking part in a mad, exuberant game of football with the boys in the courtyard. The stark lights from the windows of the orphanage cast bizarre shadows onto the ground in what seemed like a cruel parody of the floodlit pitch. Bassas produced a pocket Olympus and began to take photos, with both Darren and Utrillo breaking off to pose with groups of the boys, in a bizarre epilogue to their visit.

The drive back through Tirana's dark and largely

deserted streets provided ample time and an apt back-drop for Darren's burden, otherwise he'd end up like Utrillo: so stuffed with good causes and political postures he could barely move. But equally, it was no longer possible to say you didn't belong to the real world, to say that your entertainment of the masses was enough. Darren tried to find a middle route through this unfamiliar landscape. Perhaps the simplest guideline, he concluded, was that where events or incidents impinged directly onto his life, then he could, and should, do something to help. In the case of the orphanage, Darren felt that his involvement was perfectly justified.

The first test of this belief came as soon as he and Utrillo got back to the hotel, making their way through the kitchens and into the dining-room in time for the seven o'clock call. But as they came in, to find the rest of the squad seated at the long table, they could see in the faces of their colleagues that something was amiss.

'Sorry, are we late for dinner?' Darren asked.

From a corner of the room, Dawes appeared, eye-balls like polished stones. 'Worse than that,' he said darkly, 'you missed a team meeting!'

Darren looked at Utrillo, hoping for help. 'I called it at short notice,' Dawes continued. 'On the assumption that *all* my players would be in the hotel as instructed!'

Darren sagged. Now wasn't the time to come clean about what they'd been doing.

'Look, it's my fault . . . I just fancied a bit of air . . .'

Now Utrillo stepped between Darren and Dawes. 'No, it's mine. I asked Darren to join me . . .'

Dawes gave Utrillo a cruel smile. 'Well you'll be joining him on the subs' bench tomorrow night! Give you a chance to work out how big your fines will be!'

Darren made a move towards Dawes but all this

164

prompted was the coach's fist slamming down on the table. 'You should have been here! I told you that the streets out there aren't safe!'

'They're perfectly okay, boss,' Darren said weakly.

Dawes jabbed a finger at him. 'Shut up, Darren! I don't want to hear your voice again tonight!' With that, he stalked out of the room.

Back in Barcelona, Claire was preparing dishes for a lunch party she'd organised the following day. 'Organised' was perhaps too generous. When she'd left Rafael's he'd made noises about where she would be watching the Barca match – live transmission from Albania was scheduled. The discussion then developed into an invitation to lunch. She'd arranged for Jesper Petersen's wife Utta to come over as well, partly to see what she thought of Rafael, and partly to allay any suspicion of intimacy that Darren may feel when he phoned.

Her feelings for Rafael were all over the place. She was in awe of his reputation and his success, but was also aware of a profound sexual undercurrent in their relationship. Yet even this was confused – if he'd simply wanted Claire for a one-night bunk-up, he'd had his opportunity the other night. She felt he was playing games with her, undermining Darren one minute, praising him the next. And his arche-typal seductive manner with her jarred with that of the lost-soul image still bleeding from a broken marriage.

Naturally none of this found its way into her conver-sation with Darren when he finally got through, just as Darren didn't dare ask why she hadn't been in when he'd phoned the previous night. She casually dropped in the reference to Rafael coming over for lunch, and waited for a reaction. It was difficult to discern emo-

165

tions down an echoing and crackling line, but Claire sensed a level of frostiness from Darren.

'Did he invite himself or did you invite him?' he asked. Claire said she couldn't remember, just that she and Utta Petersen were 'getting to watch the match and you know how it is'.

'Well I just hope I play well enough not to embarrass you in front of him,' Darren muttered. There was no disguising his sourness. He would have told Claire the real reason for his unhappiness, but she didn't bother to ask. That perverse element in relationships in which one partner expects the other to guess the other's inner feelings as a test of their understanding had suddenly come into play here. As they replaced their respective phones, both Claire and Darren felt a greater distance between them than half the Mediterranean was providing.

Down in the hotel lobby in Tirana, another of the evening's fractures was under attempted repair. Gamez had collared Dawes as he sat in what passed for the lounge of the hotel. Word had come through about Dawes's earlier tantrum and the disciplinary action taken against Darren and Utrillo.

'I would prefer for there to be no publicity about the fines, Kenny. It should be a private matter.'

'Be hard. Players gossip. Press pick it up. Soon gets around, Roberto.'

'We can deny it. This is a minor incident away from home. Doesn't seem as though there were any women or drinking involved.'

Dawes snorted. 'With Utrillo it could be a Lesbian Teetotal Collective!'

Gamez sat forward earnestly. 'And I think you should reinstate both players into the team.'

Dawes's face darkened. His authority was being undermined yet again. 'Senor Vice-President,' he said attempting as much formality as he could muster, 'the rest of the squad have heard me discipline these two players. I can't go back on it.'

Beads of sweat were forming on Gamez's upper lip. 'But to leave them out for this game would cause much speculation!'

'Injuries in training,' Dawes said, trying to cajole him with a wink.

'Kenny, look, this is my first game in charge overseas . . .'

'Ah. And you'd prefer a quiet time and 5–0 win?'

'Exactly. If President Vaqueras gets angry, then we are all at risk.'

'I'll see what I can do,' Dawes lied.

Gamez wiped his lip with his handkerchief. 'That won't be good enough. I want you to do what I tell you!'

Dawes smiled implacably. He could handle Gamez because he'd shown his weakness. Dawes stood and walked off to the staircase, without saying another word.

The following morning, Gamez found himself summoned to a pre-breakfast meeting by both Darren and Utrillo. They had decided that the reason for their absence from the team meeting should be made clear, and that their proposal for helping the orphanage should be discussed immediately. They both knew that it would have little chance of acceptance once the match was over and the squad was back in Barcelona. The disciplinary action which Dawes had taken also gave them the ideal negotiating weapon – dangerous publicity.

Gamez suffered agonies as Utrillo unveiled his plan for Barca to provide humanitarian aid for the benighted orphanage. Utrillo spoke in English, to enable Darren to understand the precise terms.

'What I propose is that Futbol Club Barcelona will give the receipts for the return leg of the tie at Nou Camp to the Albanian Red Cross, who will then repair and furnish this and other such orphanages . . .'

Gamez ran his fingers through his hair in exasperation. 'I cannot endorse this, Manuel. This is a renegade action. The subject of a disciplinary stand by Dawes!'

'But the two issues can be kept separate,' said Darren. 'What would the procedure be for this proposal?'

Gamez felt himself being ambushed. 'It would have to go before the club's general committee. And UEFA would need to be consulted.'

'Surely it's a private matter for the club?' Darren asked, piling on the pressure.

'It's not that simple, Darren. Say you are a Barca fan who pays his money for a game, assuming that the money will be used for the good of the club. We are breaking our unwritten "contract" with him.'

'But what is your personal feeling?' Utrillo persisted.

'I have a few problems with it as an individual. As Vice-President, I can see many more. If we do such a thing once, will it be expected again? We'll be asked why we don't give money to poor *Catalan* children. Have you made a commitment yet to the man who runs the orphanage!'

'Not in precise terms, no.'

'Good,' said Gamez with finality. 'Because I would prefer you to forget all about it. We cannot let Dawes know what you've been doing – he would try to ban you for a month! So please, stop it. Stop it now!'

Darren and Utrillo looked at one another, wondering what their next move might be, and what damage it might do to them. In the short-term, Dawes stuck by his decision to demote both players to the substitutes' bench for the match against Dinamo Tirana. The television audience back in Spain was treated to the sight of two of Barca's star players trooping along the touchline in their track-suits while the team warmed up on the pitch. Indeed, it was such a shock, that the mobile camera concentrated on the expressionless faces of Utrillo and Darren as they took their seats, rather than on the pre-match action on the field of play.

Claire had the sound turned off on the TV set which she'd moved through to the kitchen for her lunch with Rafael and Utta Petersen. And while she concentrated on the last-minute preparations and Utta laid out the table, the silent pictures of Darren's humiliation passed unnoticed.

'Should we decide on some kind of code now?' Utta asked Claire with a suggestive smile. 'About whether you want me to stay, or for when it's time for me to go?'

Claire admonished her quickly. 'Stop putting ideas into my head!'

Utta was about to reply when she saw the pictures on the television. 'Claire – look at that!'

Claire saw the big close-up of Darren as the camera went in search of reaction from the two relegated players.

'Looks like Darren and Manuel are only substitutes!'

Claire turned the sound up with the remote control and soon heard the rapid-fire chatter of an excited Spanish commentator. It was too fast for her.

'Can you catch any of this?'

'They're saying something about it being a bizarre decision by the coach . . .'

'I wonder what the hell's going on?'

The doorbell sounded. Claire went out into the hall and opened the door. Rafael was there, accompanied

169

by a rather handsome male friend. Rafael kissed Claire on both cheeks.

'Claire, this is a friend of mine, Emilio Canillas, one of our best young architects and designers.'

'Hi . . .' Claire said, distracted both by Darren's predicament, and this latest move of Rafael's. Could he really be bringing a friend along as 'protection'?

'Pleased to meet you, Claire. Rafael has been speaking very highly of you,' Emilio said pleasantly, prompting another thought in Claire's mind – was Emilio Rafael's 'second opinion' on Claire?

'Come on through,' she urged rather brusquely. 'Sorry – we've just been trying to work out why Darren's on the subs' bench . . .'

'No! He can't be!' Rafael exclaimed excitedly as he made straight for the television. 'The fans will not like this – Darren is already a big hero. If Barca lose because of this, Dawes will not be allowed back in the city!' And after brief introductions to Utta, the two men settled down with attention only on the match now in progress.

For Darren and Utrillo, watching the game was an abstract experience. The passion and frenzy of the Albanian team's early attacks were matched by the noise from the home crowd, and closer to, the loud calls from Dawes to 'Stay awake!' It all swirled around them, barely touching them, such is the state of limbo of any player made substitute.

Gradually the game assumed a quieter tone as Barca's defence began to solidify and find its bearings. Dawes sat down and stopped twitching.

Back in Barcelona itself, Claire was able to get her guests to the lunch table and lower the volume of the TV set. They were even able to start up a conversation, as Darren's problems receded from the immediate reality. Until, that is, the phone in the kitchen rang. It was Nick Young calling from his office in London.

'Hello, darlin' – now look, what's occurring? I've just punched up the teletext to try and get the latest score, and I find that my major client has been dropped to the subs' bench! So just tell Darren I'll catch the first flight out tomorrow morning and sort this out, okay? *Ciao*, or whatever it is . . .'

Claire hung up the phone, trying to reconcile the effects of all this instant information criss-crossing Europe. The lunch was now assuming a surreal quality: civilised conversation about design matters mingled with pithy observations about Barca's timid play. Occasionally Claire would catch sight of Darren on the screen, sitting impassively, his eyes avoiding the camera's gaze. It felt like she hardly knew him at all.

The match finally took a bizarre twist of its own when the Tirana team scored from a corner-kick which the Barca defence couldn't clear properly. Thunderflashes and lurid flares were let off by the Albanian crowd as a guttural roar of celebration echoed around the stadium.

Dawes was very nearly apoplectic, screaming a near incomprehensible stream of expletives at his team. He kicked out at a plastic bucket containing the cold-water sponge, spraying the rest of the dug-out. Now he approached Darren with his teeth bared.

'Right then, dickhead – you got us into this, you get us out!'

He gestured for Darren to warm up, and he instantly set off down the touchline on a run, jinking right and left to get his legs working. Now the substitute had been transformed. Like a sudden new character on the stage, he was an instrument of drama. Unfortunately for Darren, the storyline took a turn for the worse soon after his arrival on the pitch.

He had been chasing, as he was now so used to doing,

a long-ball dropping on the edge of the Tirana penalty area. His first touch was good, allowing him to take the ball past a defender who was still off-balance. The next defender threw himself into a premature attempt at a block, but Darren took the ball round him too, and had drawn his right foot back to shoot when the goalkeeper dived at his legs and brought him down. Penalty!

Darren lifted himself up, brushed off the tufts of dried grass and walked back after placing the ball on the penalty spot. He could almost feel the TV cameras around the pitch being trained on his face. He took a breath and charged the ball, hitting a thunderous shot . . . just over the bar.

Claire turned the television off as soon as the final whistle sounded, obliterating the caption 'Dinamo Tirana 1 FC Barcelona 0' and stilling the rabid laments of the commentators. She wished she was on her own.

'I advise you not to let Darren see the papers for the next few days,' Rafael said quietly.

'What about *my* old man?' Utta cried out. 'He played in this disaster! My week is going to be fun too!'

Emilio began to collect the plates from the table.

'It was a wonderful lunch anyway, Claire.'

'Thanks. Please – leave all that to me, Emilio.'

Emilio and Rafael shared a look. Did they have *their* 'code' worked out too? If they did, it worked quickly, because Emilio announced he had to go and offered Utta a lift.

'No, thanks, I only live a few blocks away,' Utta said, looking to Claire for any signals.

'I can finish up here,' Claire said flatly. There was a brief exchange of handshakes, kisses and 'see you again' farewells, before Claire found herself alone in the house with Rafael. She felt very peculiar. It was the first time she had ever experienced embarrassment watching Darren play football. Perhaps it was just the new setting, the intense television exposure, the attention of other people that had caused it.

'I should go too,' Rafael said softly.

But Claire found herself answering, 'No, it's okay.'

Rafael looked at her. She returned his gaze. She wasn't sure what she wanted to happen, but was doing nothing to stop it. Rafael moved gently towards her and touched her cheek with his hand. He lifted her face up to him and began to kiss Claire with a slow, but intense passion. Claire broke away.

'Please . . .'

Rafael looked at her quizzically. All the questions had appeared answered a few moments ago. Now there were more?

'I'm not interested . . . in . . . in one-night stands,' Claire said defensively.

'Neither am I, Claire.' Rafael stared at her and smiled sympathetically. 'Give yourself time . . .' he said, and then he left.

The fall-out from Barca's defeat, even in this comparatively trivial away leg of a European tie, proved to be substantial. The airport, in the dead of night, provided an ominous prologue, as the squad and officials trooped out from the Arrivals lounge to find a clutch of Barca supporters whistling their derision, and two news-crews training cameras on them for reactions. Darren and Dawes, the two main targets, bustled past, heads low. Darren at least was able to fall back on a phrase he'd been working on, which he'd felt might come in useful – '*No tengo nada que decir*.' But Dawes could only spout its English equivalent, 'No comment.' The coach took the tired and deflated players back to the ground, whence they dispersed in taxis and cars to the sanctuary of their homes.

In the halflight of his kitchen, Darren poured out the

remains of a bottle of brandy into a tall glass. He opened a cupboard to dump the bottle and saw three empty wine and two empty mineral water bottles already stacked. He took a slug of his drink. Behind him, Claire wandered in sleepily, wearing a long T-shirt.

'What time is it?' she asked, rubbing her eyes.

'Late. Early. Who knows?' Darren's voice was expressionless.

Claire came over to him and tried to snuggle up to him for comfort, but he slipped out of her arms and continued to down his brandy.

'I saw the game. What happened?' she asked sympathetically.

'To me, or the team?'

'You, of course!'

'I don't want to talk about it.' Darren finished his drink and walked back to the sink to place the glass on the drainer. He opened the door to the waste cupboard.

'Got through quite a bit of wine . . .'

'I told you Petersen's wife was coming over too. And Rafael brought a mate of his.'

'Let me guess, another designer?' He gave Claire an ironic smile.

'Well, yes, but interiors rather than clothes . . .'

'Pity he wasn't out in Albania. Could have given him some work . . .' Darren didn't clarify the reference. He looked at Claire coldly. 'So – a jolly afternoon then?'

'Talking fashion, with one eye on the match. Bit of a letdown, wasn't it?'

Darren was stung. He glared at Claire. 'Oh, I'm so sorry I got dropped and missed a penalty and we lost to a bunch of part-timers! We ruined your day obviously!'

'Darren!'

He began to stalk the room, the anger that had been held in finding articulation through the drink. 'Bloody designers! If you stand still for one minute in this city, somebody will incorporate you into his latest bar, or disco, or atrium or frigging theme restaurant!'

Claire took the insult personally. She wasn't prepared to indulge him just because he'd lost a poxy match.

'It's one of the main reasons I find life here tolerable, actually – the creative eye.'

Darren's face contorted with contempt. 'Creative eye, my arse! It's a wank, Claire. One big wank. All that money spent on shower units you need an engineering degree to operate; on washbasins you can't get your head into 'cos the tap pokes your eyes out; I mean we've got toilets with seats the shape of the Olympic Stadium when my bum isn't! The triumph of style over substance!'

Claire stared at him disbelievingly. She'd never, *ever* seen him like this before. Angry, yes, but that was usually expressed in petty, almost comical tantrums. This was different. He'd found something to hate.

'Does that include my work too? Not that you ever bothered to give it more than a passing look. What's this about, Darren?'

He held to the frame of the sink, composing himself. He turned to her, speaking quietly now.

'I've seen thirty kids stuffed into a room without a single bed or radiator! One hole in the floor for a toilet, and one in the ceiling for a shower. What we spend in one supermarket trip would probably keep them going for a month . . .'

'Tell me about it,' Claire pleaded.

'You wouldn't understand,' he said dismissively.

Now it was Claire's turn to retaliate with malice.

'I understand one thing – you missed that penalty on purpose didn't you?'

'Don't be bloody stupid . . .'

175

'I could tell by your eyes . . .'

'I'm surprised you had time to look!'

'*Why*, Darren?'

He brushed past Claire and headed upstairs. Later Claire went in to him but he was flat out, exhausted, sleeping noiselessly. When he woke somewhere near noon the next morning, Claire wasn't in the house. In the evening they sat more or less silent through a quick meal and a rented video. Whatever was eating into Darren wasn't up for discussion. But then neither was Claire's increasing fascination with Rafael.

When the players next reported for training, Darren and Utrillo gathered them into a group and told them what had happened in Albania. They explained their plan for raising funds for the orphanage, and Gamez's opposition to it. It had now become a matter of honour for both men, but they knew they could go no further without the backing of the rest of the squad. Darren proposed a simple vote – '*Para los ninos – si, o no?*' As the players looked at one another, waiting for a cue, they were propelled into a 'yes' vote by a decisive gesture from Vila. This seemed quite bizarre coming from the squad's self-absorbed playboy. But then Darren knew more about him now.

With their comprehensive mandate for action, Darren and Utrillo sought an immediate audience with President Vaqueras and Vice-President Gamez on the President's opulent suite deep inside the stadium. Their first ploy, an attacking one, was to reveal that a journalist had accompanied them on the 'illicit' trip to the orphanage.

'We cannot therefore guarantee that the story of our visit will not be revealed,' Darren stated.

'Which journalist?' Vaqueras enquired coldly. He knew them all, of course. But was better acquainted

176

with their editors. Utrillo was only too aware of this. He gave Vaqueras a defiant smile.

'We cannot reveal his name . . . but I think if our proposal is rejected he might well link the story of our fines to the club's reluctance to support the orphanage.'

'This sounds like blackmail to me!' shouted Gamez, sensing that the whole Tirana affair was bound to condemn his prospects for the Presidency.

'Really? Since when did players have such power?' Utrillo asked ironically.

Darren sat forward. 'We should point out that the entire squad has backed us. We will give up our match fees for the return leg as well. If you decide not to donate the club's takings . . .' Darren shrugged like a Mafia godfather, letting the silence do the work.

Gamez stared at him wildly. 'You're presenting us with a *fait accompli*! We cannot accept this!'

But Vaqueras, ever the diplomat, had registered the determination of the two players. As he saw it, he had a choice between damage limitation, or turning the incident to the club's advantage. He calmed Gamez with a gesture.

'This club is a great institution. We should never forget that. I think we have to put our faith in our public. Tell them the truth. There is one thing above all which Catalonia knows about, and that is suffering.'

It was the move of a supreme fixer. By devolving any 'decision' to the public – by which he really meant the press and radio – Vaqueras could be seen in a neutral position, ready to lend his support in whichever direction the club was taken. But the key mention of the word 'suffering' suggested that, in his head, Vaqueras knew that a great publicity coup was available to him.

The negotiations between Dawes and Nick Young were not so straightforward. Nick had, as promised, flown over to Barcelona to have a word, anxious for the rift between Darren and Dawes to be healed. He caught up with Dawes on the training pitch, with the players already gone to the dressing-rooms. Even so, Dawes insisted they should walk away from any possible eavesdropping. Dawes seemed utterly intransigent about the matter.

'Nick, he was out of order. And *you're* out of order coming over here to make it an issue.'

'I'm trying to *prevent* it becoming an issue. Darren was led astray. This Utrillo geezer's a real Trot, isn't he?'

'Don't I know it!' Dawes exclaimed.

'Darren just went along, with the best of intentions . . .'

'No, he didn't. He knew something like that would be a stirring job!'

'Will the club accept their proposal?'

'If they do, it's gonna make me look more of a shmuck, isn't it? I fine two players for indiscipline and they wind up getting the bleeding Nobel Peace Prize?'

'How can we square it with you?' Nick asked diplomatically. A bit of grovelling was always necessary if it looked like the gravy train was about to be derailed.

'I want Darren to admit he was wrong *and* to take his fine like a man. If he won't do both, I'll leave him out of the team.'

This didn't seem to leave much margin for negotiation. 'Can we talk about it over lunch?'

'You're joking! I'd have to get you to taste the food to see if it was poisoned after that result!'

'You realise that the tabloid Rotters will have a beano over this. They're just dying to see Darren come a cropper.'

Now this really was stony ground – appealing on the basis that his client could be savaged by the press. Dawes smirked at Nick contemptuously. 'Tough. I'm not his PR. If he puts his hands up and pays without squealing, we're sweet.'

Those were the terms Nick would have to take back to Darren. But Dawes had one last accusation to make.

'I'm sure he missed that penalty deliberately, you know?'

Nick looked at him incredulously. 'Nah! Don't be daft!'

Over the next few days, it became apparent that the Catalan media and the fans, via telephone polls, were much in favour of the club donating its revenue from the return leg of the tie to the Albanian orphanage. Darren and Utrillo gave extensive briefings to press, television and radio, and soon a considerable fund was building for transfer to the Red Cross. His involvement in the campaign gave Darren a new sense of worth and an inner strength to face whatever Dawes might throw at him. When they eventually met in his office, with Gamez and Nick Young as mediators, Darren was mentally prepared for the worst of Dawes's threats.

Dawes staked out his ground immediately. He'd been outflanked by the public support for the donations, but that hadn't altered his opinion that there was a disciplinary issue outstanding.

'If you want me to make a statement backing down, then I'll quit.'

'Please. Listen.' Gamez turned to Darren and nodded.

'I'm sorry, boss. I was in the wrong. For the right reasons, but definitely in the wrong,' Darren said calmly.

'Was that an apology?' Dawes asked, sensing a lack of genuine contrition.

'He'll be backing your decision on the local news

179

tonight. And agreeing to pay the fine in full,' Nick added.

'What about Utrillo?'

'The same,' said Gamez.

'We're getting somewhere . . .' said Dawes, smiling.

'The President backs you also,' Gamez reported.

Dawes faked horror. 'Now I'm worried!'

'And it was his suggestion,' Gamez continued, 'that the club donate the fines also to the orphanage fund . . .'

Dawes winced. 'That leaves you smelling sweeter than me! But then that is the general idea!'

'The idea is for harmony to be restored,' Gamez said impatiently, barely able to disguise his self-interest.

'What if I don't pick Darren for the next game?' Dawes asked mischievously.

Gamez gave him a stern look. 'President Vaqueras has asked for more goals . . .'

Dawes thought for a moment. On balance, he'd got a result. 'I was only kidding!'

Darren was duly restored to the team for the next league game, and also lined up against Dinamo Tirana in the home leg of Barca's European Cup tie. Before the match, he joined Utrillo and Vila in a ceremony on the pitch for the benefit of the press and television cameras. Myftar from the orphanage had been flown to Barcelona, and was now presented with a money-order and two dozen junior-sized Barca kits. Myftar, Vila, Utrillo and Darren embraced for the cameras in a gesture of unashamed brotherhood. This didn't prevent Darren scoring a hat-trick against the Albanian team, however, as Barca swept to a facile 3–0 win, winning the tie on a 3–1 aggregate.

While the Tirana incident had enlightened and empowered Darren, there was one area of his life over which he had lost control – Claire. A chasm of misunderstanding and silence had formed between them over her professional efforts, while he sensed in her, if he was honest, an emotional drift towards Rafael. He didn't have the time or energy to confront this, with the result that when Claire took her completed designs round to Rafael's studio while Darren was playing in the Tirana match, it took on the appearance of a symbolic act.

Rafael picked up on it, of course. He praised Claire's first designs, but cautioned that she would have to be bolder to make them distinctive.

'Bolder. Yes. I think I'm getting there,' Claire said with a knowing smile. Rafael crossed to his 1950s American fridge and pulled out a bottle of vintage French champagne to celebrate Claire's first success. As he twisted the cork off, Claire reminded him of an earlier discussion.

'I don't need drink to make my mind up, remember?'

Rafael stared at her, knowing that the moment was now right. They drank the champagne anyway before climbing up to his bed which looked out over the rooftops of old Barcelona. Rafael insisted, half-jokingly, in having the broadcast of the match on while they were in bed. Far from perverse Claire found it utterly cathartic to be made love to by a sensitive, strong, passionate man, while in the background, the Spanish commentators twittered their inane observations about such a little matter as a football match.

Chapter Nine

Having learnt, during what the Barcelona papers called 'The Orphanage Affair', that the press could be a useful weapon in his survival armoury, Darren now set about enlisting their support in his remaining battle – to convince Kenny Dawes that there was no future in the pragmatic, defensive-minded football which he was forcing upon the Barca squad. Darren had dithered for some time over this issue, which had been confused, ironically, by his own success at scoring goals regularly. He had also been wary about being manipulated by the team captain Utrillo into the position of 'front-man' for the frustration the twenty-man squad was feeling.

But now, after a particularly tetchy training session, in which he had been loudly bollocked by Dawes for 'not working hard enough', Darren had resolved to strike out on his own. From a purely selfish viewpoint, he could see that he was becoming the team's workhorse, too often the only point of attack, always the first line of defence. The copious mental and physical energy these roles demanded was draining him of his basic enthusiasm for the game. It was only a matter of time before he became a victim of the system and was dropped from the team. It was time to act.

The daily gathering of press at the perimeter fence round the training pitch – every nuance of form, dissent, skill, fatigue found its way into the next day's papers – provided him with the opportunity. Pressed for comment on his deteriorating relationship with the coach, Darren had responded with a deadpan 'No comment'. But he was able, as he squeezed into his car, to give the nod to Jordi Bassas, the journalist who had become his friend and confidant during 'The Orphanage Affair', for a private 'briefing' back at his house.

Darren waited by the pool with his diminishing six-pack for Bassas to arrive, which he duly did over the garden wall.

'Sorry, Darren. There are a couple of the other press boys out on the street,' Bassas said by way of apology for his unusual arrival.

'I know. My doorbell thinks it's at a Catholic wedding . . . well, bollocks to them. You're the only local journalist I trust . . . in fact, delete local.'

He handed Bassas a San Miguel.

'*Muchas gracias* . . . I am honoured! Now you want some cash for this?' Bassas asked for openers. Darren waved his hand dismissively.

'No, no, Jordi – this is a freebie.'

'Sure?'

Darren nodded decisively. 'No direct quotes mind – just "It is believed that Matthews feels . . ." and "Close friends of Matthews say" . . . Is that okay for you?'

Bassas laughed. 'I am used to this – before sport I did politics.' He took a small tape-recorder from his jacket. Darren winced. 'Do you mind doing notes? Tapes have a habit of falling into the wrong hands.'

Bassas laid the tape aside, flicked open a notepad and clicked his pen in readiness. 'Ready when you are, Darren.'

Darren took a long swig on his bottle. 'This has been coming to a head for a while. I'm not happy with the system we play. Nor are most of the team. I don't expect the fans are either, are they?'

Bassas shrugged. 'Barca are second in the League and Real Madrid fourth,' he said, referring to the lasting enmity between the two sets of fans, 'so for now they are okay. But if it becomes the other way round . . .'

'Well, anyway, I get the feeling that the crowd's not excited about us. We're an efficient side. Hard to beat. But there's no beauty in our play, is there? No magic. No fantasy.'

'What about the tension between you and Dawes? You seemed to be arguing today . . .'

'Yes, because he knew you press-guys were there! It was all designed to make me look the guilty party. Believe me, Jordi, I'm not a moaner, but Dawes is so obsessed with this pressing game, he forgets about the need for individual skill!'

'Do you think it would be better for you to have a partner alongside you, helping you?'

Darren allowed himself a wry, private smile.

'Yeah, and on the pitch too.'

'Sorry?'

Darren's private life had no place in the papers so he cut quickly to answering the original question. 'Yes, I definitely need someone else for me to play off. Can't do anything without the ball, can I?'

Darren drained the bottle and then forlornly tossed it into the swimming pool. He watched it sink slowly into the pale blue water, giving him an instant, finishing image.

'So – do you think you can help Dawes get the message?'

Claire and Rafael had repaired to the shower after a languorous afternoon of love-making, which the context of her new work-place made readily available. Rafael towelled her dry, relishing another chance to stroke her body.

'I can't bear the thought of you going home to Darren,' he said suddenly. This possessive thought disturbed Claire. They had yet to confront any of the ugly implications of their affair, and Claire wanted to keep it that way until she was more sure of her feelings, and more secure in her working relationship with Rafael.

'Well I can't leave him. Not yet. Not just like that,' she said, as if stating a universal truth.

'Why not?'

'Because we came out here *together*. We've helped each other through a lot. All right, we've grown apart in the process, but . . . I know he still needs me.'

'But you're ready to spread your wings, Claire. You can't let him hold you back!'

'We're two Brits in a strange city. It's not that easy to pull ourselves apart.'

'So what am I then?' he asked petulantly. 'Just someone who sees you when you have some free time from Darren?'

Claire kissed his chest in answer. 'No, you're very special.'

'Then prove it to me. Darren is a man. He can live without you. A Barca footballer can have any girl he wants in this city . . .'

Claire leant on Rafael, comforted by his strength but worried by his ardour.

'What if he only wants me though?'

When she arrived back at the house, she became instantly aware of a strange atmosphere. Music was blasting from the stereo – a track by the Flamenco rock group Pata Negra to which Darren had become partial. She made her way down to the kitchen. Darren was at the stove, cooking messily, and singing along in passable Spanish. She watched him for a moment; it was obvious that he was pissed. She felt a natural fondness swell inside her.

'Finally worked out how to switch the cooker on?' Darren stopped singing and turned to her. 'What's brought this on?' she asked with a smile.

Darren showed her his recipe book, *Floyd on Spain*, a present sent by a friend back in England.

'Cooking for piss-heads in three easy stages,' Darren said, slurring slightly. '*Gambas y pimentos con samaina!*'

Claire smiled again. Then his mood changed in an instant. 'Thought I'd better get some practice in.'

She avoided his challenging look, and went out to switch off the stereo before returning.

'Have you been drinking?'

'All afternoon. And I plan to keep going.'

Claire approached him cautiously. 'What's the matter, Darren?'

He feigned renewed interest in the copper pan on the stove, stirring the bubbling liquid.

'You're giving up on the workroom upstairs, are you?'

'For the time being, yes. It's easier if I work at Rafael's . . . starting to get some of the pieces made up now.'

'Great. I hope you're still hungry . . .'

'*Still?*' Claire asked with a frown.

'Well, I assumed you'd gone out for lunch. There was no answer when I phoned the studio this afternoon.'

Claire blinked. 'We just went round the corner for a bite. What time's dinner?'

''Bout half an hour. Want to invite him round?'

'Who?' she asked, desperately treading water.

'Your new boss . . . partner . . . whatever he is?'

Claire could sense the drift of the conversation. It was dangerous. She didn't want this now.

'Rafael's buying my designs. That makes him a client,' she said firmly.

'Client, eh? And what are you exactly?'

Claire turned and headed out to avoid confrontation.

'I'm going upstairs to change . . .'

As she went into their bedroom, peeling off her top, she froze. All the drawers in her bedroom furniture had been pulled out and their contents scattered onto the floor. A gnawing sense of dread rose within her. She jumped with fright as Darren ran his index finger up her bare back.

'No scratch-marks. Good at following orders, is he?'

Claire shied away from him, covering herself up, as if being confronted by a stranger. She pulled her top back on.

'What are my clothes doing on the floor?'

'For the second time today, no doubt . . .' Darren said with an unpleasant leer. Claire tried to push past him.

'I don't have to put up with this . . .'

Darren grabbed her by the shoulders and pushed her back on the bed.

'Darren!'

'Jog your memory, does it, being on your back?'

'Piss off!'

'Want to know why your clothes are out? Because you may as well start packing . . .'

Claire struggled beneath him. 'Why?'

Darren snarled at her. 'Because I don't want you here any more! Go and shack up with him – that's what you want, isn't it?'

'You're the one who's driving me out! Look, Darren, if you want a serious discussion about our relationship, I want *you* sober and *me* fully dressed!'

187

'And Anna bloody Raeburn officiating?'

'We don't need outside advice on this. Just common sense . . .' She broke off, sniffing dramatically. 'What's that smell?'

'Stop trying to distract me . . . I want a straight . . .'

'Burning . . . there's something burning!'

Claire wriggled free and jumped off the bed, hurtling out of the room. Darren followed in a daze.

Downstairs the kitchen was filling with smoke. The pan on the stove had caught fire and flashes of flame licked upwards.

'Shitty death!' Darren yelled. He yanked a small fire-extinguisher from its wall-bracket and struggled to prepare it for firing.

'Take the yellow tab off!'

'Where, where? The instructions are in German! Right! Got it!' Darren advanced on the pan and pressed the switch on the extinguisher. Foam shot out drowning the flames and swamping the cooker. Claire wafted away the smoke and opened the door onto the garden. Darren turned the cooker off and backed away, suddenly sober.

'That's the last time I try Keith Floyd . . . he's a fucking fire hazard, that guy!'

Claire started to giggle. Darren couldn't help but laugh out loud, expelling the tension from his frame.

'I've a good mind to make you eat it now!' he gasped.

'Come on, we need some fresh air . . .' Claire said, taking his hand.

They took a taxi down to the harbour where the breezes from the sea washed the smoke and the bitterness from them. They were calm now. Anger was spent. They walked along the harbour wall, side by side, like a nervous couple on a first date.

'What do you want from me, Darren?'

'I suppose at the moment I want you not to be sleeping with your designer friend . . .'

Darren watched for the effects of his words on Claire. No denial came.

'I'll put it down as a score-draw then, shall I?'

Claire looked at him, feeling his suffering.

'This isn't about revenge, Darren.'

Darren saw the remoteness in her eyes. He knew then he had lost her. 'Christ, it's serious, isn't it?'

'Can you imagine what it's like for a woman to be involved with a footballer. Trying to convince herself that everything's all right? That there won't be a crowd of girls hanging round the team hotel? That her man isn't a sexual fantasy figure for thousands of teenage jail-bait?'

'I'm over all that stuff now. The lads are serious about the job here. It matters more.'

'Ah, that's the secret is it, money?' she asked with cutting irony.

'I meant, it matters in terms of who you are and how people see you. You're trusted here. Respected. Looked up to. Being a footballer's a . . . commitment . . . a sort of responsibility. In England, the bosses and the press would rather keep us in a state of permanent adolescence. Because it's easier to deal with us that way. Daft, cock-happy lads, unable to believe their luck. Unable to grow up till it's too late.'

He looked at her – there were still no signs of regret, not a glimmer of encouragement. He felt his stomach churn. 'It *is* too late, isn't it?'

She said nothing, avoiding his look.

'*Why*, Claire? I've always tried to support your career . . .'

Claire gave him a pained smile. 'You were only ever interested in the *idea* of me being a designer, Darren. You never believed in the reality. Rafael *does*.'

189

'But why *fall* for him?' he asked plaintively, butchering himself inside.

'I'm not sure myself yet. We've both changed over here, Darren. We're not the people we were back in England.'

'You mean I'm no longer good enough for you?'

'I'd prefer to see it as "no longer right".' She paused. 'Just as I'm not right for you.'

'Who says? *Who* says?' he demanded.

'Well, if you must know . . . my heart.'

They stopped and faced one another. Darren made a sweep with his arm round the harbour, lit by the sunset over the mountains. He could hardly believe paradise could be this poisoned.

'I'd swap all of this to keep you!'

Claire took his hand. 'Your job's to be the best centre-forward in Europe. To make this city remember you.'

'How do I do all that without you?' There were tears in his eyes now.

'You've got everything going for you here, Darren. You don't *need* me to make a success of it. You don't even think that yourself, do you? Be honest.'

'I don't know *what* to think at the moment, Claire. To fight for you, or shake hands and wish you a nice life?'

'Something in between, I'd have thought. If we're sensible, we can survive this, you know.'

They had dinner at one of the smart fish restaurants overlooking the harbour. The air was warm and all around them families and couples chatted happily. Darren felt as if he was in a surreal parody of a romantic supper. He stored every detail, every second of their time now, as though he was rescuing treasured possessions from a burning house.

When they returned home, they lay together on top

of the bed, fully clothed, talking in staccato bursts of shared nostalgia as they down-loaded the memories of their relationship. The curtains at the window fluttered in the breeze, revealing glimpses of the night sky. Occasionally sleep ambushed them, sometimes separately, sometimes together.

'I remember feeling like this once on a school coach trip to Weymouth. Car-sickness, I suppose,' he muttered.

'Flattering to the end,' she said, kissing his forehead like a nurse.

'Disorientated. Like my stomach's outside my body.'

'Queasy – that's a good word. I remember your mother using it once, when I first came round for tea. Ham sandwiches with the crusts cut off, and the room full of pot-pourri air-freshener.'

'You had a shiny green dress on.'

Later, Darren woke from a sleep. Claire was watching him still.

'Have you noticed how footballers keep coming up with the phrase "It hasn't sunk in yet" when they're asked about a success or a defeat? I mean, we prepare every inch of our mind and body for either, but then when it happens, we can't find a way to express it properly.'

'You didn't get that off John Motson. What brought it to mind?'

Darren grimaced self-mockingly. 'The "unsunk-inness" of tonight, I suppose. The fact that this is probably the last time you and I will ever lie next to one another.'

'Remember when we bought our first double bed? You wanted to stretch out on it for an hour in the window of Maples?'

Darren smiled at the memory. 'It's getting light. Do you fancy a cup of tea?'

'No, thanks. I must get some sleep.'

'Did I drop off before?'

'Somebody was snoring, and it wasn't me.'

'Just one of the many things you'll miss about me.'

Darren felt his eyelids close and his body grow twice as heavy. When he woke several hours later, Claire had gone. He placed his hand on the still-warm part of the bed where she had lain.

After nearly three months in the job, Kenny Dawes was still living in a hotel, albeit a five-star one. He'd rationalised it long ago, but now as he escorted his latest female companion out of the lift and kissed her goodbye, he felt a pang of longing for a home, for a family-life again. It was early days – the woman he'd met several weeks ago was divorced, and still bruised. But she was nice to him. And it felt good having a regular companion. In a few weeks' time, he'd have a look at some of the smart villas in Darren's vicinity. Set up a home for himself and see if she was interested.

He strolled jauntily into the breakfast room and took his usual table. The maître d'hotel scurried over.

'Sorry, Senor Dawes, still no bacon, I'm afraid.'

'Just the usual then,' Dawes said with a cheery smile. And then he caught sight of the newspaper a businessman was reading at a nearby table. There was a picture of himself and Darren, arguing head-to-head in the previous day's training session. He could make out the headline above it: '*Los Ingleses a Guerra!*'

'Carles, do you know what that paper's saying about me?' he asked, pointing across. Carles winced.

'I don't think you should read it on an empty stomach, Senor Dawes!'

Darren staggered groggily down the hall as the doorbell rang insistently. Now there was a hand pounding against the door itself. He was still wearing the clothes he'd slept in. He heaved open the door. Kenny Dawes was standing on the top step, holding a newspaper which he now thrust at Darren.

'You little shitbag, Darren!' he shouted.

Darren tried to order his thoughts. 'What?'

'I've been well tucked-up in this! "The English at War!", that's what that says. And that's the politest bit!'

'Look, boss, this is a bad time . . .'

'Bad time? Is there a *good* one to be told what a turd you are?'

Dawes looked Darren up and down. He thought he recognised the dishevelled look. 'Been out all night spending the backhander you got for shafting me?'

'That's not the way it is.'

'Don't give me that bullshit, son! I know how it works. You think it's new? Players were at it in my day too. The only difference being that the managers I played under in the sixties would have taken you behind the stand and given you a kicking for squealing to the press! If you don't like the way I run the team, you tell me to my face. Understand?'

'I've tried but I can never get through!'

Dawes whacked Darren across the face with the rolled-up paper. 'Well, you have now!'

Darren had summoned sufficient consciousness to retaliate now. 'Come off it! You knew the press were there yesterday. You were just trying to make me look small. To get your own back for the last time!'

'I've very nearly had enough of you, Darren! I want you to stay away from training until I work out what to do about you. You don't look fit for it anyway!'

'Why don't you *listen*, Kenny? That's all you have to do!'

Dawes was heading back to his car now. 'You're out of the team, Darren! O-U-T. *Out!*'

193

Dawes climbed into his car, slammed the door and drove off, scattering gravel everywhere. Darren rested his head against the architrave and closed his eyes.

An hour later, he'd packed a bag quickly and cabbed it to the airport for the first flight back to London. It wasn't an instinctive, foetal reaction. He'd just reasoned that it would be best for him to be out of the way for a few days, while Dawes's temper cooled off and the Barcelona press exhausted the story.

So within three hours of his row with Dawes, he was walking out of Terminal 1 at Heathrow, wearing dark glasses and the previous night's stubble as a temporary disguise. The sounding of a horn alerted him to the presence of Nick Young's car, which was cruising the parking lane in an attempt to defeat the attentions of the ever-eager airport traffic wardens. Darren clambered in and Nick pulled sharply away and headed for the M4 and London.

Darren looked out of the window as the car joined the motorway, and ran straight into the coned-off lane. The traffic was tailing back and drivers all around were having heart-bursting tantrums. It was a grey, lowering kind of day, and the bleached out scrub on the edge of the worn-out motorway seemed like images of the England he'd forgotten. Nick waited patiently for an explanation for this sudden return.

'Forgotten your mother-tongue, have we?' he asked acidly.

'I don't want to talk about it.'

'You ring me up to tell me you're flying into London, giving me about two hours' notice, and all I get is silence!'

Darren remained silent despite the provocation. With the traffic now at a standstill, Nick had the chance to look him up and down.

'What's with the stubble?'

194

'I didn't shave,' Darren said blankly.

'Darren! What's going on here? Brain damage?'

Darren sighed heavily and took off his sun-glasses.

'Another ruck with Dawes. I arranged for him to be slagged off a bit in the press. Now I'm out of the team and banned from training.'

'Terrific. You go to a new country, handle the language, the people, the food, but you can't get on with the only other Brit at the club! There's a word for that!'

'Unlucky?' suggested Darren.

'*Perverse*. The story'll be over here by tomorrow, you know? The Single European Market applies just as much to football gossip as it does to M & S underpants.'

'I'm planning to lie low with my mum and dad for a few days.'

'I'll do my best to keep the Rotters off you. Want me to call Kenny?'

'No, no, you'll be wasting your time. I just hope it doesn't blow things for me over there.'

'He's got a terrible temper, but he forgives eventually,' Nick said reassuringly. 'Claire not with you?'

Darren turned away to look out of the window again. 'That's another story.'

'Yeah?'

Darren said nothing. 'That was a "yeah" as in "tell me more".'

'And this is a "no" meaning "not yet".'

The traffic started to move again, apart from the guy on the inner lane who'd fallen asleep at the wheel. 'Lucky bastard' thought Darren.

They stopped off in West London to pick up a hire-car for Darren, with Nick negotiating a cut-price VIP deal for a Mondeo.

'Fine,' said Darren. 'Don't really want anything that gets me looked at . . .'

'Time for a quick lunch?'

Darren shrugged. Nick had never seen him so subdued, and decided a little sympathy might not go amiss.

'From your dog-faced demeanour I take it this is a serious spat?'

Darren was hardly listening, his mind was back in Barcelona. 'Terminal, I'd say. Been coming for a while, mind. We don't really get on any more.'

'Well it was always a risk, if you ask me. Two volatile, strong-headed people.'

'The thing about being abroad is, that you can't walk away from it. You're forced together.'

'Are you sure there's nothing I can do?'

Darren frowned at him. 'Such as?'

'Well, alert the European transfer market to your possible availability . . .'

Darren groped to work out when the misunderstanding had set in. 'I was talking about me and Claire. Not me and Kenny Dawes.'

Nick exhaled in exasperation. 'I thought you *weren't* going to talk about it! Well there's *definitely* nothing I can do there. Come on.'

They moved out of the car-hire compound back towards the main street. Nick continued with his 'write-off' of Darren's relationship with Claire. 'And to be honest, provided she doesn't try and grab a slice of your wages, or shop you to the Rotters, I'm not that interested!'

'Thanks,' Darren said. 'There'll be none of that anyway. She'd never dump on me.'

'Never say "never" where the press and a jilted bird are concerned.'

'It's her who's elbowing me, actually.'

Nick shook his head. 'Gawd – now I know she's bonkers! Right, well just be careful, eh? You're gonna look a right loser if this gets out.'

Darren darkened. '*Loser?*'

'Well, you know. Rich young footballer, enjoying life with one of the best clubs in the world and this bint walks out on you. Bound to be questions asked.'

'What?'

'Well, about whether you've been using her as a punchbag.'

Darren pulled at his stubble for comfort. 'We've just agreed to go our separate ways, that's all.'

'Doesn't sound like you had much choice! I suggest you find someone closer to your speed next time, more used to life in the fast lane.'

Darren laughed sarcastically. 'What's this – relationship advice from the man who'd define infinity as the time between him coming and the woman going?'

'I'm a man of experience, Darren. I know the wiles of the enemy!'

At least this brought Darren a crumb of amusement. 'Nick Young – Agony Uncle? All the subtlety of a Benetton advert.'

They turned the corner to the street where Nick had parked. His face suddenly contorted with rage. His car was being hoisted onto a tow-away truck. Nick burst into a sprint.

'You fascist bastards, I'm trying to get this country's economy moving!'

After a nasty pub lunch – oh, how Darren missed all those arrays of fresh tapas he'd grown used to – he collected the car and was off up the M40. At least the new bit hadn't crumbled away yet. An hour later, he was cruising through the streets of his home town, feeling as though he'd just woken up from a dream. All that sunshine, the luxury home, the fast car, the acclaim of the Barcelona fans – now here he was, back to earth.

He made his way through to the 'executive-style' home that he and Claire had planned to move into and pulled up outside. It was complete now. All the external finishing – gardens, picket fence, tarmac drive – was in place and there were frilly lace curtains hung in the windows.

He'd persuaded his mum and dad to move in there while he was away, imagining initially that one day he'd be back to claim it. Now he felt he'd rather die than move back. He looked at it, trying to imagine the nerd he once must have been to have seen this property as the symbol of his success. John Major's hilarious 1992 election broadcast came to mind.

'It's still there!' he mimicked in a nasal drone. 'It's *still* there!'

Lil was home. He'd taken the precaution of calling her from the airport so that she didn't die of shock when she saw him coming up the garden path. Unfortunately, she'd also taken the call as a cue to prepare his favourite dinner. Darren sat, pinned down by despair, in the lumpy, maple armchair as she swung in from the kitchen with a tray. And it was only five o'clock!

'Here you are, Darren – liver casserole!' She thrust the tray onto him and sat down awaiting compliments.

'Mum – what about the dining-room?'

'And risk scratching that fancy table?' Lil tutted.

'Mum, I own it. It's for eating your dinner off.'

He began to eat the shapeless brown sludge on the plate, faking appreciative noises for her benefit.

'What time do you have your tea out there? All we saw of you was parties!'

'Well, if you'd stayed a bit longer, you'd have found out a bit more . . . we eat about ten normally.'

'Ten? You can't get to sleep till well after midnight!'

Darren was grateful for the conversation, it meant he didn't have to eat for a few more minutes.

'Well, the Spanish get up a bit later. Have lunch about two. Go back to work about five. Knock off at

198

eight for a few drinks and tapas . . . they're little snacks
. . . then have dinner late. They get more out of the
day, that way.'

Lil pulled a face. 'What a palaver. No wonder nothing gets done in Spain.'

'What about the Olympics . . . and the Expo in
Sevilla?'

She scowled again and got up. 'Right, I'll go and
wake your dad, and get him ready for work . . .'

Darren saw his chance. 'Ee . . . the man works all
night, sleeps all day . . . has a pint at six in the morning.
That's no way to live!'

Lil eyed him as only a mother can. 'Have less,
Darren. Or you won't stay the prodigal too long.'

She went to the door of the lounge, but was determined to have one more go.

'By the way, it's Seville in this house not Sevilla,
thank you very much!'

She went out. Darren wished the technology existed
for him to be elsewhere immediately.

Chapter Ten

Darren drove his dad down to the meat market on the outskirts of town that night, in time for starting his evening shift. The conversation didn't exactly flow. Freddie could sense the smell of failure hanging over his son and didn't want to know what was behind it. Darren was happy with that too. He still felt the burden of Freddie's expectations regarding getting into the England team. Until such time as this elevation came, he knew that the move to Barcelona would be regarded by Freddie at best as an unfortunate error, at worst as a betrayal of his country in favour of a lorry-load of Spanish pesetas.

Darren parked inside the main gates of the market complex and Freddie nodded for him to walk up to the main hall with him. They set off past the convoy of humming refrigerated juggernauts waiting for their supply of carcasses. It was a walk Darren had done many times as a lad, and it felt vaguely reassuring to do it one more time as a successful footballer.

'Maybe we can christen that snooker table of yours over the weekend?' Freddie said cautiously.

Darren shook his head at the realisation that his father had yet to use this expensive toy which Darren had bequeathed to him when he left for Spain.

'You always said it'd be the last word in luxury. So when you get one, you don't use it!'

'Well, it's never felt right. Playing in your own home. Well, *your* home. We've not settled too well, to be honest, Darren. It's all too modern for us – microwaves, underfloor heating, security systems, satellite TV. Like being on "Tomorrow's World".'

'It's *today's* world, Dad.'

'I don't mean to be ungrateful, son, but we'd like to try and get a house back near the old one if possible.'

'I gave you the house so you and Mum could share in some of my success! And now you want to move back?'

Freddie stopped walking and took a long hard look at Darren, trying to imagine what had happened to the obedient little boy who'd done this walk so many times before.

'At least we had neighbours there! And there was a pub just a walk away! And a corner shop! This place of yours is cut off from the rest of the city. Like you were ashamed of it, or something!'

'A footballer's entitled to his privacy, you know, Dad.'

'Your mum reckons it's all gone to your head. That you're too big for your boots . . .' Freddie grinned at stumbling upon a pun, '. . . so to speak.'

'Here we go – the English disease. You mustn't let success change you! What's the bloody point of succeeding if it *doesn't* change you? If it doesn't make your life easier; if it doesn't widen your horizons? How else would you *measure* success if these things didn't happen?'

Freddie looked alarmed by the outburst. His Darren never used to be like this. 'No need to fly off the handle!'

But Darren hadn't finished. 'It's not like this in Spain, you know. You're not crippled for life by being born into the wrong class!'

Darren's shoulders began to sag. He ran his right

hand through his hair. 'Sorry . . . I've been under a lot of strain the last few days. Claire and I have split up.'

Freddie hung his head. 'Oh – oh, dear. Sorry, son. Not much I can say, really. Never been much good at talking about that sort of thing.'

'I know, that's why I'm telling *you*, rather than Mum. Break it to her after I've gone back, will you? I don't think I could face one of her lectures at the moment.'

'What went wrong then . . . that business with the other girl?'

Darren shook his head. 'I think it's more to do with what happens when you step out of the familiar rut of things. You know, when you're with somebody through habit rather than choice.' Darren gave a fatalistic shrug. 'In a new country, you don't have habits, so you're freer to choose.'

Freddie nodded. He sort of knew what Darren was getting at, but after a life spent in captivity, with only work, a wife and son, and a steady routine as companions he couldn't really grasp the full sense. 'I'll take your word for it.' He offered Darren his hand to shake. Darren thought about hugging him, but was sure Freddie wouldn't understand the gesture.

'See you later then,' Darren said taking his father's hand. Freddie walked and disappeared into the macabre business of the meat market, the only world he really understood. Darren shivered, and headed back to the car.

Rather than go back home, he drove into town and dropped into one of his old haunts, a wine bar in the university district. The people who ran it knew Darren, and with a clientele mainly consisting of students, he knew he'd be less likely to get any aggro from resentful locals. Indeed, after a few exchanges of news with the proprietors and a couple of old faces Darren was able to install himself at the quiet end of the bar and enjoy an undisturbed drink.

Until, that is, he heard a familiar female voice behind him asking, 'Didn't you used to be Darren Matthews?'

He knew who it was before he turned – Jane, his ex-lover, who'd shopped him to the tabloids when he'd moved to Spain with Claire instead of her. Because it was a Friday night, she was dressed to the nines. Darren gave her a cautious smile.

'Don't worry, I'll go in a sec. I just wanted to say I was sorry for what I did.'

'I think, on balance, I deserved it, don't you?'

Jane took this as evidence of forgiveness, and rather than rejoin her friends, stood her ground.

'What are you doing over?'

'Flying visit.'

Jane made a play of looking around behind Darren. 'Claire not with you?'

'She's . . . er . . . not well.'

'Nothing trivial, I hope,' Jane said cruelly. It was the first sign of bitterness.

'Why are you angry with *her*, Jane? It was me who shat on you.'

'What do you do when you lose a game, Darren? Blame the ball, or the opposition?' Darren stayed quiet, hoping the subject would go away. 'You can buy me a drink, you know. I'm over eighteen.'

Darren signalled to a barman for two more glasses of wine. Jane took this as her cue to move onto the stool next to Darren, taking off her jacket to reveal a low-cut, backless dress. Darren couldn't pretend he didn't notice it.

'That's new.'

Jane flicked back her long blonde hair, confident now that she had Darren's attention. 'Made a few bob out of the story. Got me a few modelling jobs as well. Had to rebuild my life a bit, didn't I?'

Darren paid for the wine and passed a glass to Jane.

203

'You never really expected me to dump Claire, did you?'

Jane pantomimed confusion. 'Sorry, Darren, it was *you* panting on my doorstep at every available opportunity, wasn't it? It was *you* who told me I had the best body you'd ever seen?'

This was all true, another reminder of his confused and often sordid past. 'Yeah, all right . . .' he conceded.

'So why should I have believed your bloody relationship with her was going to last? Claire wanted one thing out of you – a leg up on the fashion ladder, that's all!'

Darren couldn't stop himself smiling ruefully. 'Well she's certainly got that.'

Jane stared at him as the realisation sank in. A smile of victory spread across her face. 'She's dumped you, hasn't she?' Darren took a long sip from his wine glass to avoid answering. 'I hate to say I told you so . . . but I just *knew* you two weren't right for one another,' Jane crowed.

'Please. Can we leave it?'

'You need looking after – you know that?' Jane said in a sudden moment of calculated tenderness. She put her hand onto the small of Darren's back.

They had a few more glasses of wine, a bite to eat at the bar, and three coffees each. Nothing much was said, except for Jane trying desperately to get a picture of the life-style in Spain. By eleven, Jane's friends had long since gone on to the disco. So it fell to Darren to drive her home. He was dreading the moment when he pulled up outside her flat. He began to see it not so much as a crossroads but as a motorway intersection in his life. He knew what she'd say, but what he didn't know, in his tired and vulnerable state, was what his reply might be.

After he parked, they both sat there rather self-

204

consciously for a moment, waiting for the other to say something. Eventually Jane said the inevitable.

'Do you want to come in then?'

Darren tried hard to cling to what he instinctively felt. 'Better not.'

'We could make up for lost time . . .' She was planting the old images in his head, of all the fantasies she'd made come true for him up there in that bedroom just thirty seconds away.

'I don't think so somehow,' he said quietly.

'Just think what we could do with a whole night together.'

He did think, he *was* thinking. Snapshots of their exotic love-making flashed into his mind. God it would be so easy just to give her his body for tonight. But he knew it wouldn't be that simple. It wouldn't end there. She'd be flying back with him if she could. That would complicate his life and probably fuck up hers too. If there was one thing he'd found out about himself in Spain it was that the judgement of his cock wasn't to be trusted. That there was a life of the mind as well. He took a breath and cleared his head of temptation.

'Jane, you don't understand. It's all in the past now – Claire, you, this city. England.'

'You can't just leave your life behind like that.'

Darren turned to her with a look of a wild determination in his eyes. 'Watch me!'

Jane opened the car door. 'I'm not going to hang around, Darren. I know what I've got to offer. If you don't want it, I'll find somebody who does.'

She closed the car door and strutted across the pavement to the door of her flat. Darren watched her go and then rested his head on the steering wheel.

Darren's absence in Barcelona had been noted by now. The evening sports news on the Catalan station TV3, had been full of lurid stories of the suspension of the Barca star, complete with a reporter door-stepping his house and getting no answer. This had prompted an anxious Claire to ask Rafael to drive her over to the house.

'I'm sure you're worrying over nothing, Claire. Players are used to these sort of setbacks . . .' Rafael said, more in self-interest than in reassurance.

'Yeah, I know – but on top of everything else . . . I'll just check he's okay.'

Rafael stayed in his car as Claire let herself into the house. Inside, it was in darkness. Claire walked round switching lights on but there was no sign of Darren.

When she came back to the car ten minutes later, she seemed still preoccupied. 'His passport's not there. Must have gone home, I guess.'

Rafael suffered. There was always this point in the transfer of relationships where guilt and concern over the previous lover threatened to alienate the new one.

'You have to cut off, Claire. It's no good bringing an old relationship into a new one.'

He drove off abruptly and they continued in silence for a while, before he suggested dinner at a small, intimate restaurant in Sant Gervasi. It did the trick. Claire emerged more reassured than she had been and was touched by Rafael's patience. They walked to the car arm-in-arm.

'I'm sure that once Darren is over the shock he will throw himself into his football.'

Claire nodded her agreement. 'I just hope he doesn't sink under the weight of it all.'

Rafael pulled her close. 'Claire, he's not your burden. Not any more.' Claire rested her head on his chest, and he kissed it gently. By the next morning, Claire had reprocessed more emotional waste into a non-toxic alternative.

She and Rafael took breakfast at one of the pavement cafés in the beautiful Placa Reial, complete with fountains and colonnades. Rafael checked through the sports pages for the continuing news of Darren's dispute with Dawes.

'I've been thinking . . .' Claire volunteered. 'Maybe I *should* move my stuff out . . . it's not fair on Darren, me hanging on.'

'It's not fair on *yourself*, Claire. You cannot lead two lives.' Claire nodded her agreement. 'Don't you think it's more than a coincidence that Darren should go away like this? He *wants* you to move out. He's trying to make it easier for you, by not being there.'

Claire frowned. She hadn't seen that. 'Then why not let me know?'

'He *has* done . . .' suggested Rafael. He gestured to the papers. There were photos of Darren and Dawes all over the sports pages, and a headline which translated as "Darren Flees Barca".'

Darren slept late, his body weighted down by the strain and fatigue of the past few days. He was woken brusquely by the loud shouting of his mother outside the bedroom door.

'Darren – wake up!'

He stirred groggily, wondering where the hell he was. Now Lil burst in throwing the door back on its hinges.

'It was bad enough when that trollop had you all over the papers. Now there's about five reporters on the bloody doorstep!'

Nick had been right. There were no frontiers for sports scandals these days.

'Tell 'em to piss off!' he retaliated.

'Did you know they were going to chase you here? Hey?' Lil poked him through the duvet before stomping out. 'Life was never like this before you moved!'

Darren pulled the duvet over his head and burrowed down as far as he could for sanctuary.

When he surfaced an hour or so later, the hacks had disappeared, convinced that the trail had gone cold. Darren took a shower and then shaved off the two-day stubble which was in danger of becoming a token of self-pity. The fact that he'd been able to resist Jane's dangerous fruits also cheered him. He decided he'd go and watch his old team play, as they had a home game that afternoon.

As he approached the small, rather tatty stadium, hemmed in by rows of houses, Darren felt his exile from Barca even more sharply. He drove into the club car-park, attracting obscene gestures from a few still resentful fans. He signed a handful of autographs as he made his way across to the entrance, where he was greeted with apparent affection by the commissionaires and stewards. Only when he headed off for the home dressing-room did one of them say what most of them were thinking after the stories in the press. 'I knew he wouldn't last out there.'

The players were more genuinely welcoming, calling him 'El Golden Bollocks', asking about his life-style and moaning about the fact that, thanks to the bloated English football calendar, they'd probably played about a dozen games more than Darren in exactly the same time-span. It was good rough and tumble stuff, reinforcing Darren's view that though the fittings and fixtures were dramatically inferior, there wasn't that much difference in spirit between this dressing-room and Barca's.

What a difference upstairs in the directors' box though – the same old self-satisfied faces, in the same seats, all thinking the same way. The club chairman, Derek Horsfield, was still wearing two-tone shirts. Didn't anyone have the courage to tell him that the eighties were over?

The match was complete crap. Lots of high balls and crunching tackles, and Darren began to notice just how many touches these Premier League players needed to control the ball – three, four, five! Most of the people he was playing with at Barca took instant control for granted. It was the first skill they had learnt and the one they kept most sharply honed. This made him even more depressed about what Kenny Dawes was doing to the team – another few months and they'd look like one of these teams out here today, thought Darren.

And then it turned nasty. The home side conceded a soft goal from a corner – old habits die hard – and there was a distinct restlessness in the crowd. Some of the fans in the enclosure in front of the directors' box had already spotted Darren arriving and jeered at him. Now they quickly orchestrated a vengeful chorus of 'Who's the bastard in the stand?', jabbing their fingers at Darren the Great Traitor. Darren sunk lower into his seat as the chant continued and the inevitability of a home defeat became obvious.

Derek Horsfield was full of apologies after the match, when he invited Darren into the directors' lounge as his guest. Darren reflected that it had taken a £1.5 million transfer to finally gain him entry into this holy-of-holies.

'Sorry about the abuse. It's normally reserved for me,' Horsfield said, pouring Darren a beer he hadn't asked for.

'Only to be expected. Some of them will never forgive me for leaving. A win today might have helped things.'

'Yeah, but then you'd only have got . . .' Horsfield slipped easily into an oafish tone, ' "You shoulda stayed at home" from The Mensa End.' He raised his glass in a toast to Darren. 'Sorry to read about your trouble with Dawes.'

'It happens.'

'If you fancy coming back, you know . . .' Horsfield said, not quite playfully enough.

'Can't see it, actually. Didn't think you had any of the money you got for me left anyway?'

'I beg your pardon?'

'What happened to the one-and-a-half million you got for me? I don't see any new players. Any new facilities.'

Horsfield bristled with indignation. An ex-player, voicing an opinion. The only crime more heinous would be for a current player to do it.

'We *have* halved the overdraft, Darren! Not that it's any of your business anyway. Nor the fans'.'

'Did you know that Barcelona's stadium was built with subscriptions from the fans? That it's a club, where the supporters have membership? That the President and the Committee are all elected by the membership?'

He might as well have been speaking Swahili for all the effect this had on Horsfield. Darren couldn't stand the atmosphere in the lounge any more.

'Never learn, will you . . . ?' he added to Horsfield before giving him the beer glass back and leaving.

This was a big mistake. The crowds were still making their way home, so Darren took a whole lot more obscenity when hostile fans – and they were wearing the home colours – pressed their faces against the window and made 'wanker' gestures at him, before gobbing onto the windshield.

When he broke free of this mob, he was slowed by the phalanx of visiting supporters being escorted to the station by mounted policemen. The car was passed by a hot-dog trolley, trundling its greasy way back to some lock-up in a railway arch. An ambulance now sped past in the opposite direction, heading for the ground, blue lights flashing. And there, as he pulled clear of the

210

stadium and its human detritus, were a clutch of supporters joyfully pissing against a garden wall.

Darren needed sanctuary. He headed straight for Alfredo's restaurant. It wouldn't be open yet, but the ebullient Anglo-Italian would be in his kitchens making his seafood sauce. He'd be delighted to see Darren. They could share a bottle of vintage Barolo and catch up with all the football gossip.

The restaurant was in darkness as Darren approached, but after he'd parked and gone up to the door, Darren saw that it wasn't due to pre-opening preparations. All the furniture inside had gone. The windows were streaked with dust, and a pile of junk-mail lay unopened on the floor. On the inside of the door's glass panel was sellotaped a yellowing note of thanks to all customers from Alfredo, together with apologies for ceasing trading.

Darren drove back to London the following morning, dumped the car and flew back to Barcelona in the afternoon. His mood had been bleak before coming to England, but now it was as cheerful as a Siberian winter. He couldn't face the prospect of a return to English football now. He'd finally seen how much it had excluded the fans and the players from its administration, and gone slobbering in pursuit of spiv money. Someone had once called English football 'The People's Game', but it never had been and now it never would.

Nor did it console him, when he took a taxi in from Barcelona Airport, to hear on the radio that Barca were trailing 0–1 at home in their League match. An untried teenage forward had been brought in as replacement for Darren. The tone of the radio commentator was shrill and critical. The taxi-driver turned to give Darren his verdict on the team – a thumbs-down gesture. But

Darren felt no pleasure in this, only more determination to make Dawes see the way ahead.

As the taxi pulled into the drive of Darren's house, he saw Rafael's red Honda sports parked outside. He went into the house cautiously, dreading the thought of a confrontation, and fearing what he might do if pushed over the edge.

Claire was in the hall, kneeling down as she folded clothes into a suitcase. There were two others already packed.

'Darren! God – sorry. Didn't expect you back.'

'Is he here?' Darren asked tetchily.

'No, no – he lent me his car. He's gone to the Barca match . . .'

'You'd better get ready to give him a good time then – they're getting beat!'

Claire stood up. 'I thought it would be a good idea to get a few of my things while you were out of town . . .'

'Sorry, I couldn't find anything to keep me at home any longer.'

'Read about your bust-up with Dawes. The papers here have been full of it . . . one of them's running a telephone poll to see who's right – you or him.'

Darren allowed himself a bleak smile. 'What a circus, eh?'

'I'm sorry – it's all you needed . . .'

He shrugged. 'A defeat today would help . . .'

'Pity that it has to come to that.'

'Well I've got no future back home. And I need a bit of luck to make things work here.'

Claire moved towards him. 'Look, Darren, I don't want you to go to pieces over us . . .'

' "Go to pieces"? Well, I'm hurt but I'm not cracking up. There – you're off the hook.'

'I beg your pardon?'

Darren spelt it out for her. 'I don't intend to burden

212

you with guilt by throwing a wobbler or by wrecking my career at Barcelona.'

'How did you reach this conclusion?'

'There's nothing like a weekend at home to make you appreciate life overseas. Made me realise how lucky I was to have got here, and how I shouldn't let it slip away.'

'That's good.' Claire looked into his eyes to check that this wasn't just bravado. 'Are you sure you're all right?'

He smiled for her benefit. 'Sure. "The smile is my make-up, I wear since my break up, with you . . ."'

'"Tracks of my Tears", right?'

Darren nodded, then suddenly began to sag with the accumulated stress. Claire moved close to comfort him. They held each other.

'We know so much about each other's lives. That's what I can't stand losing. It's like my past is being eaten up behind me faster than I can move.'

'Go and see Dawes first thing tomorrow. Clear the air. Get your football right, and the rest will follow.' Claire stroked his head affectionately not amorously. 'You can make it, Darren. You have to look on this like . . . like shedding a layer of skin. The reason things get left behind is because you don't need them any more!'

Darren composed himself. 'Right – I'll give you a hand out with this lot, shall I?'

He loaded up the car for Claire and then stood outside and watched her go out of his life. Tomorrow had to be a new start, in more ways than one.

Indeed, during an early morning, lung-busting run up to Tibidabo, from where he could see a magnificent sunrise over the sea, Darren pumped himself, perhaps a little artificially, with self-belief. He felt like 'The Little Engine' – 'I-know-I-can-play-I-think-I-should'.

After showering, he drove over to Kenny Dawes's

213

hotel to try and see him and solve the dispute between them. The reception clerk directed Darren up to the roof-top pool where Dawes would be taking his daily swim.

Dawes was breast-stroking his way slowly up and down the pool. Darren stood at one end, waiting to be spotted. He soon was. Dawes came thrashing to a halt and clung to the edge of the pool, looking up at Darren with a glower.

'Go on – take a piss on me, why don't you? Everybody else has this morning,' Dawes said, referring no doubt to press reaction to the previous day's defeat.

'I think we should have a talk,' Darren said calmly.

'I daren't go out without a bag on my head,' Dawes joked. Only he wasn't joking. He clambered from the pool, wrapped himself in a towelling robe, and led Darren across to the breakfast counter. They took plates of fruit and pastries, and big cups of coffee before seating themselves on loungers.

'First up – I apologise for what I did. I was completely out of order. I know the Spanish lads have been putting me up to it for a while, but this was my own doing. There was no excuse for going to the paper.'

'I want whatever you got donated to charity – a little stroke I learned from you.'

'I asked for and got nothing, boss. Promise. I was trying to make a point, not score some dosh.'

'Suddenly you're a man of honour? Listen, Darren, you've crapped on me two or three times now. What makes you think an apology is going to put things right?'

'It's a start, I hope. Look, I doubt if any of this would have happened if Claire and I hadn't split up.'

'I thought you were rock solid? Well, I'm sorry, son. But you have to learn to put things like that to one side. Not let it affect your game.'

214

'I'm *trying*, believe me. But there's nothing I can do about it if I can't get back into the team.'

'You must have been hooting when we got beat last night,' Dawes probed, looking for sympathy.

'Look, we both need some quick damage limitation work. I'll make my apology public. Make sure the President gets to hear about it. Get the press off our backs.'

'It's not going to be that easy, Darren! In English terms, we have brought the club into disrepute!'

'Put me back in the team, boss!' Darren said plaintively. 'Let me make a fresh start. Put the kid up front with me. Push Cuipers out wide from midfield, and we'll have a good 4–3–3!'

'Suddenly *you're* the manager?' Dawes said sharply.

Darren drooped again – it was like beating against a rock with bare hands. Dawes looked at him, and suddenly, he softened. 'Must be a bit tough having a break-up abroad?'

'Yeah. The only people we could talk about it with were ourselves.'

'I've got myself a little lady,' Dawes confessed, somewhat sheepishly given his previous record of cash transactions. 'Separated, mind. Works in a bank. Steady. A change for me.'

Darren smiled. He'd never seen Dawes so human.

'You're settling in a bit more then?'

'Until you started undermining my bleedin' job, Darren!'

'Boss – can we work together? You know, with one purpose? Make the team more exciting?'

'I'll think about it. No promises though.'

Darren stood up. This had been a good start, and he didn't want to push his luck.

'I'll see you tomorrow morning then . . .'

'You'll see me this afternoon,' Dawes said with a wink. Darren was puzzled.

215

'You don't really think I'd give the team a day off after a 1–0 home defeat?'

Darren slapped his forehead in mock recrimination – he really should know Dawes better by now.

When he got to the ground Darren found Dawes waiting for him in the main entrance. They had a meeting with the President in his rooms. This consisted largely of the two Brits grovelling in apology for their all-too-public spats. Darren convinced Vaqueras that their mistakes were born of ignorance not of intent, which was a lie, but sounded grand and diplomatic. Vaqueras seemed to accept it all, provided they made statements to the press about their reconciliation, and provided Dawes spoke in Spanish.

They all shook hands at the end, with Vaqueras expressing a hope that the team's morale and form would now improve. Dawes and Darren both uttered platitudes and left, completely convinced that they had, in footballing parlance, 'got a result'.

The afternoon's training session therefore took on the feel of a celebration, as Dawes restructured the line-up into a more attacking formation. Darren loved it – he had less running to do, and still saw much more of the ball. As he slammed home his third goal of the practice match, after a sweet passing move, he 'aeroplaned' across to Dawes, inviting him to slap one of his outstretched palms. He did, but still wanted this new style tested in the combat of a real match.

The training sessions for that week were therefore geared to 'bedding in' the new 4–3–3 formation, with Darren joined up front by the teenager Padrol and the Dutchman Cuipers. The players felt liberated by the change, like prisoners who'd had their diets changed from bread and water to asparagus and salmon.

The good humour was spoilt, however, by the arrival

216

of Jordi Bassas on his 250 cc moped. Dawes saw him and stepped in straight-away.

'He's *banned*, Darren! I don't want him around the ground!'

Bassas ran across excitedly. 'This is urgent for you too, Senor Dawes!' he said breathlessly.

Darren and Dawes shared a look of anxiety. 'What is it? If I let you speak, it's on condition that it's in front of me,' Dawes snapped.

Bassas shifted uneasily on his worn-out sneakers.

'Go on, Jordi – Kenny and I are all sweetness and light now.'

Bassas nodded, and took a breath. 'Exactly one hour ago, the President of Barca meets two men from a Montevideo flight . . .'

Dawes looked blank. Darren supplied the geography lesson.

'Uruguay, right?'

'*Si*. One is Hugo Barresco . . .'

'The South American Footballer of the Year?' Darren asked anxiously.

'*Si*. The other is his manager.'

'You mean his *boss*?' Dawes queried with alarm.

'No, no, his agent! The word on the street is that Barca will sign Barresco tomorrow!'

Bassas winced as he said it, knowing the effect it would have on Darren.

'Looks like you're for the chop, Darren . . .' Dawes guessed, taking the worst interpretation.

Darren took it too. It looked like he and Kenny had kissed and made up far too late for President Vaqueras.

Chapter Eleven

With the formal signing of Hugo Barresco taking place at the Nou Camp Stadium, Darren and Kenny Dawes carefully absented themselves from their place of work for an afternoon on the golf course. There was no point in Dawes attending, since all the sporting press knew that club president Vaqueras had signed Barresco without consulting Dawes at all. And had Darren been spotted by the Spanish journalists, they'd have bombarded him with questions about his future now that a star international forward had been bought by the club. So Dawes's lush country club golf course, just down the coast from Barcelona, was the right place to be, not least because it gave the two Englishmen the chance to plot their survival in Spain in private. Dawes aired his anxieties first.

'I've just settled in here. Just got the feel of the place. And now this! I *know* about these South American glamour-boys. Whenever they move, they bring their coach with them like a security blanket! It's only a matter of time!'

Dawes prepared for his next shot, screening his eyes so that he could see the green ahead.

'So what are you going to do?' Darren asked, leaving golf etiquette to one side.

'Less of the "you", please, *kemo sabay*,' Dawes snapped, twitching his 6-iron over the ball. '*We* are in this together! We will have to protect each other's backs!'

'But we have separate battles to fight!' Darren pointed out, suspicious of Dawes's sudden conversion to an advanced concept like loyalty.

'And they'll be a lot easier if we team up. Us against them. And then there's the other ingredient . . .'

'Which is?'

Dawes abandoned his shot and handed his club to Darren, apparently dissatisfied with his assessment of the distance to the green.

'Get my 4-iron out will you, Darren?'

Darren turned and wandered back to the golf trolley. While his back was turned, Dawes kicked his ball a foot or so out of the semi-rough where it lay and onto the edge of the fairway.

'We also have to be prepared to play dirty!' said Dawes, resuming his theme. Darren returned with the club. He eyed Dawes's ball with amused suspicion, but said nothing.

Later, when they adjourned to the sun-drenched terrace of the clubhouse for drinks, Dawes made Darren shake hands on an unofficial pact, the terms of which could be loosely summed up as 'we are Brits and we reserve the right to do anything necessary in order to pull through this particular crisis'.

'We should get Nick Young out here pronto too. We'll need his kind of low cunning on our side,' Dawes said with relish. Darren had a terrible moment of dread trying to imagine what Nick and Kenny would dream up in any undercover campaign against F.C. Barcelona. Privately, Darren preferred a football solution to any problems created for them by the arrival of Barresco – in other words, if Darren could get goals, and Dawes could get the team playing more attractively, nothing Barresco did could threaten them, surely?

But the following morning, Darren found out precisely what they would be up against as the arrival of South America's most glamorous footballer began to have its effect. To begin with, private security guards had been laid on to keep the fans back from the slope which overlooked the training pitch, in anticipation of Barresco's arrival.

The Barca squad were already on the pitch, working their way through their warm-up and stretch routines, so vital in preventing debilitating strains and pulled muscles. Dawes supervised proceedings, coaxing the players in the monosyllabic Spanish which he'd begun to adopt since the President's last warning. Every little helped, Dawes hoped.

Soon the players became aware of a buzz among the crowd of would-be watchers. A large black limo was speeding across the stadium car-park and heading up to the entrance to the training pitch. Darren and Vila had their legs spread wide and were bending to touch their ankles. Designed to prevent hamstring pulls, this particular exercise now afforded them an upside view of events as the limo crunched to a halt by the gate. The first thing they saw was a huge, well-muscled 'minder' step out of the front of the limo. The minder opened the rear door, and the stocky figure of Barresco, wearing a Uruguayan national track-suit emerged. He was followed out of the car by another burly man in sweat-pants and T-shirt.

'Our new super-star, Stanley!' Vila said, head hanging between his legs.

'Looks more like Michael Jackson arriving for a concert.'

Dawes was determined that his session shouldn't be disrupted. It was an early opportunity to try to assert some authority over the Uruguayan and his entourage.

'No talking! *Silencio, por favor!* And eyes front, please!' Dawes grimaced as Barresco crossed onto the training pitch, shouting salutes in Spanish to his new team-mates.

'Keep stretching, you lot,' Dawes insisted. Barresco swaggered towards him. Dawes tapped his watch extravagantly. 'You're late for training, sunbeam!'

Barresco understood the gesture, though not the words.

'Senor Dawes?' he asked, pronouncing it more as 'Davez' to add insult to injury. '*El entrenador, si?*'

Dawes bristled. He considered himself much more than just 'the trainer'.

'*El jefe*, son . . . the *boss*.'

Barresco shrugged nonchalantly. Dawes gestured for him to take a place in the group of players warming up, adding a thoroughly ironic '*por favor*'. But Barresco backed away towards the burly man in the sweat-pants. His precise role now became clear as Barresco lifted his right foot into the man's hand, and folded himself into a stretch.

'He's got his own trainer!' Darren exclaimed as quietly as he could.

'All we need now is Bubbles the Chimp!' Vila said with a giggle.

Dawes brought an end to the warm-ups and set up a one-touch practice game before jogging across to try to negotiate some relevant action from Barresco, who was trotting his way along the touchline, hitting his down-turned hands with his heels. His minder and trainer remained in attendance. After a few moments of gesturing, Dawes returned to supervise the practice match while Barresco continued his own little routine. Darren managed a quick word to Dawes.

'What's up – got a note from his mum, has he?'

'Next best thing. Apparently he's been told by the

221

President to take things easy for a few days. And he's allowed to train using his own people.'

'Then in a match, he comes on in a sedan chair and carpet slippers for the last five minutes, right?'

'Please, Darren, that may not be too far from the truth.'

Now another limo joined the circus, this one belonging to President Vaqueras, who emerged smiling when his chauffeur opened his door. Dawes and Darren shared a look of foreboding as Vaqueras took a place on the touchline. Rarely did the club's most powerful individual visit the 'shop-floor' of a humdrum training session. Dawes knew something was up. Within seconds, Vaqueras had beckoned him over.

'*Cincos minutos, muchachos!*' Dawes shouted to the squad in a vain attempt to impress with his linguistic progress. The match continued as Vaqueras took Dawes on a slow walk around the pitch. It was stark, staring obvious what was coming, so Dawes at least had a chance to think about the right reaction.

'Kenny, I would like you to give Barresco a start in our next match . . .' Vaqueras said firmly.

Dawes pretended great thought by stroking his chin.

'The signing has created great interest. It would be a pity to lose the momentum it has brought . . .'

Dawes tried mild resistance, to see how severe an attack on his authority this was. 'With respect, Senor President, he has hardly trained.'

'He is a naturally fit player, I think,' Vaqueras said, making his own judgement an immediate issue. 'His energy must be saved to explode in the match.'

Dawes cleared his throat. 'What about Darren?'

Vaqueras stopped walking. He watched Darren twisting and turning in the practice. 'I hear he has split up with his girl.' Dawes nodded, wondering what the hell this had to do with the new situation. 'With that and his other recent problems, we should be sympathetic, and not expect too much from him.'

Ruthlessness couched in terms of generosity, even Dawes had to admire the guy's style. 'Anyway, I trust your judgement of course, Kenny . . .' Vaqueras finished, leaving clearly coded orders.

'*Muchas gracias*, Senor President,' Dawes said with little enthusiasm. Out of the corner of his eye, he saw Darren taking a look at them, trying to work out what was happening. In so doing, he found a pass bouncing awkwardly off his shins. Vaqueras tutted.

Once Vaqueras left, Barresco too called it a day, whizzing off in his limo but pausing strategically at the gate to wave to the adoring fans. The squad took a break, swigging down bottles of Gatorade, brought out by the coaching staff. It was a time to reflect. Utrillo could see Darren was confused. He thought it might unburden him, when he guessed aloud that Barresco was after Darren's number 9 shirt.

Darren was irritated by this suggestion. 'I thought South Americans preferred Number 10 because it was Pele's shirt number?' he said petulantly before dumping his drinks bottle into a plastic dustbin and walking off. Dawes could understand Darren's mood but business was business. He sidled up to Darren while the rest of the squad watched apprehensively.

'Don't tell me – I can guess. Vaqueras wants Barresco in instead of me?' Darren snapped.

'I'm trying to think a move ahead, Darren. If I'd said no straight up, that would have opened the trapdoor for both of us.'

'What are you trying to say, that you've dropped me in our mutual interests?'

Dawes tried to make light of the moment, hoping that Darren would too. 'You're with me!'

223

'How does that help me, boss? If I can't get a game, how do I show form to get back in the team?'

Dawes scratched his head. 'Well, you'll just have to look extra tasty in training, won't you? I'll open up a few extra sessions to the local press. You've seen Barresco – he strolls it! And that will give me the opportunity to have a go at him!'

'Where does that leave me – singing "Always look on the bright side of life!"?' Darren said witheringly.

'Trust me, Darren,' Dawes pleaded, but Darren had just about had enough.

'So much for solidarity!' He slammed a stray ball into the mesh fence surrounding the training pitch and trudged off towards the stadium dressing-rooms.

Darren thought long and hard on the drive home. He knew he couldn't rely on Kenny Dawes to rescue him from the obscurity of being a non-playing member of the first-team squad. Dawes might mean well, but when it came to the crunch, he had little power compared to the President's, and would probably be unwilling to deploy even that.

The solution lay with Darren, or rather with what Darren could get people to do for him. His first call was Jordi Bassas. Darren knew he couldn't risk using Bassas as a mouthpiece for his moans; it had backfired badly when he tried it against Dawes. To employ such tactics against Vaqueras would probably go down as high treason.

'But if you won't attack the President or Dawes or Barresco, what can I write that will help?' Bassas asked when he came round to Darren's that evening.

'It's got to be something . . . well, *away* from football, I guess. Look, this probably sounds daft, but when my dad was over here, he mentioned something about my grandfather's brother helping Catalan refugees after the Civil War.'

224

'That's it? No other details?' Bassas said with a frown.

'My dad doesn't remember. His father and the uncle are both dead. Is there any chance you could check the files in your paper?'

Bassas shrugged – this was some favour. 'Sure. But something like this will be pre-computer. It could take weeks . . .'

'Well, don't bust a gut. It's just a thought. Something to help stop me becoming the forgotten man at the club.'

'A hat-trick against Real Madrid would make you immortal!' Bassas exclaimed, speaking as a Barca fan, not as a dispassionate journalist.

'Yeah, sure. I wish. But I have to get back into the team to do that.'

Bassas stood and patted Darren reassuringly on the shoulder. 'Don't get too down, Darren. Maybe Barresco will play like a dog against Espanol on Sunday.'

'I doubt it somehow,' Darren muttered, unable to resist the depression that was creeping over him. He opened another beer as Bassas left. Several more left him lying on the sofa, trying to read the evening newspaper with little enthusiasm. The phone rang. Darren looked at it – the odds were pretty short on it being a journalist. He let it ring a few more times, then picked it up.

'*Hola* . . .' he said defensively. 'Oh . . . hello . . .' he switched. It was Claire, in another of her concerned moods. He dead-batted her emotional probing by telling her he was fine, and that he was about to eat a self-cooked supper. The bravado couldn't be sustained, however, when she suggested he went out.

'Thanks, but I don't think that's a good idea. Going out doesn't appeal much if you're a loser in this city . . .' He got the protestations he was looking for, which made them sound even more hollow. 'All right, all right . . . but that doesn't stop me *feeling* like one. Look – got to go. See you sometime . . .'

He hung up the phone. Silence filled the house once again. Now that Claire had gone, he was beginning to resent her interventions into his life. It was as though she was still trying to preserve a stake in his future, he thought cynically, just in case hers didn't work out with Rafael.

'Well, fuck her, and fuck 'em all,' he muttered bleakly. All the money, all the attention, all the luxury – they were up for that. But when it came to helping Darren, at the lowest ebb of his professional career, nobody was around.

Darren wandered out onto the terrace, switching on the lights, both in and around the swimming pool. A surreal blue glow was instantly created. Down below, the lights of the city were sparkling. He knew now what went on out there – the parties, the smart dinners, the night-clubs, the jazz bands, the girls – which made him feel morose. In a strange city, you can feel like the only person alive, and it doesn't bother you. Solitude, in those circumstances, is a badge of courage. But when you're abandoned in your own town – and that's how Darren felt about Barcelona now – it could be the loneliest feeling on earth. He could sense the heaviest, the blackest depression spreading down from his brain, crushing the light out of his body. The next second Darren threw himself, fully clothed, into the illuminated pool, and let himself sink, seeing how long he could hold his breath. Seeing if he really wanted to.

Suspended in the eerie blue silence, muffled from the street noises, the chattering cicadas and the music carried on the breeze, Darren found sudden comfort. He released a burst of air bubbles, and kicked his way up to the surface. The chill of the water had sobered

226

him instantly, and the surprise of what he had done had pulled him back from the edge. He paddled to the side of the pool and pulled himself out.

'Only joking, kiddo . . .' he reassured himself.

By Sunday, the day of the match, Darren had pulled himself round. A working life that had been a continuous cycle of triumphs and defeats, had led him to rationalise this latest development as just one of many. Indeed the footballer's natural gland of optimism had been busy pumping reassurance into him. Maybe Barresco would tire quickly. Maybe Darren could come on as sub and get the goal that counts.

The excitement around the Espanol Stadium, a small and brutal concrete bowl just a few miles from Barca's own Nou Camp, also helped Darren buzz again. The match, technically a local 'derby' and associated with the usual terms such as 'hard fought' and 'closely matched', also had other undertones. The very name Espanol was a rallying point to those Spaniards who had moved to Catalonia but who did not share the region's sense of its own importance or identity. Furthermore, in the darker past, when football had been one of the few means of public expression during the Franco regime, the Catalans had seen hard-core Espanol supporters as too aligned with fascism.

So, as the Barca team coach approached the stadium, the Espanol fans were especially vociferous.

'Quite an atmosphere,' Darren said to Vila sitting next to him.

'Local rivalry. Wait till we play Madrid next week. Then you'll really see something!'

Vila's phrase suddenly had Darren plummeting again. The matches against Real Madrid were the highlights of the year, not just because the two teams were usually the best in the league, but because the historic enmity between the two sets of fans outmatched anything between those of Barca and Espanol. The possibility of missing out on such an event catapulted Darren back into a sombre mood.

Worse was to follow. In the fevered intimacy of the pre-match dressing-room, Dawes read out his team sheet and the names of the substitutes. Darren's wasn't among them. He grabbed his club blazer and walked out. He headed up the tunnel towards the pitch. Dawes came out of the dressing-room and called him back.

'Ride out today, Darren, and then we fight back, okay?'

Darren was less than reassured. He was being nobbled from above; he sensed that. And then he *knew* it . . . 'Oh, and Darren, stay away from the dug-out will you?'

Darren wheeled round glaring at Dawes, who shifted uneasily. It was even embarrassing him.

'Look, I've been told that if the television cameras pick you up sitting there, looking miserable, it'll only provoke unwelcome comment. Sorry.'

So Darren watched the match from the anonymity of a bunch of police and club stewards in the players' tunnel. It was certainly 'hard fought' and 'closely matched', too close for Barca's comfort. But they won it. Espanol couldn't get the ball clear from a corner, and as the ball ricocheted around the penalty-box, it was Barresco who stubbed a bobbling shot into goal.

Despite the farcical nature of his goal, Barresco celebrated with an Oscar-winning performance of joy and fervour directly in front of the photographers behind the goal. He knew how to get himself into the newspapers for sure. Darren felt the only possibility now for him were the obituaries.

The following morning, Darren went out to the airport to pick up Nick Young, whom he had summoned after Dawes's plea. It seemed irrelevant now – Butros Butros Ghali, the UN supremo, would be needed to save Darren.

'Spawny goal, wasn't it?' Nick commented as they weaved their way through the car-park towards Darren's Mercedes.

'They all count. That one especially. How come you saw it?'

'Was on GMTV this morning . . . with Hugo Barresco portrayed as the new villain in your life.'

'What the hell is going on back home?'

'Well, like it or not, Darren, you are a one-man soap opera. The Gazza Factor, I suppose. The fascination of watching an accident happen in slow motion . . .'

'Is that how bad I look?'

'In the present circumstances, yeah. Let's face it, we love nothing better than to witness someone flying high coming a cropper.'

Darren laughed, it was so ridiculous. He mocked himself, feigning a Woody Allen-like neurosis. 'What about my learning the language? My international charity work? Doesn't any of that get across?'

They reached the car. 'Dullsville as far as the low end of the market is concerned. The day they leave you alone, you'll know you're a quiet success.'

'You coming out here to fight a dirty campaign will be right up their street then!' Darren exclaimed, fearing the worst.

'Trust me,' Nick said calmly.

'Every time I hear that phrase, I get more and more worried . . .'

Darren drove Nick up into Sant Gervasi for lunch, telling him on the way about commissioning Bassas to try to find a story about his great-uncle's work for Catalan refugees. Nick was baffled – his idea of a useful story would be one in which club officials were photographed in compromising positions with girls. Besides, he'd already set his own rescue plan in motion.

'Right – I have a certain Premier League manager primed to call Barcelona to make an enquiry about you,' he whispered across the table, even though the restaurant was empty.

'Where does that get me? *Transferred?* Which is exactly what I'm trying to avoid!' Darren complained tetchily.

'Listen up a minute! This will make them think twice about you. You've done pretty well out here. You've got some goals. The fans like you. The local press are on your side. If the club suddenly think you might be snatched away, they'll appreciate you more!'

This was a familiar Nick Young ploy. In theory, it was fine, provided the club really did want to hang on to the player. If they didn't, it simply presented them with a quick opportunity to smuggle the discarded individual away. Besides, there were additional complications with Barcelona.

'But Kenny Dawes sees this Barresco signing as a double-whammy to get both of us out. Any talk of me going back home just plays into their hands, doesn't it?'

'Not necessarily. Has he pulled some kind of "we're in this together" number on you?' Nick asked, having quickly analysed Darren's remark.

'Well . . . he *was* coming on all Three Musketeer-ish. Maybe that's why I found his sword in my back yesterday!'

'Fair enough, then. We dump him,' Nick said firmly.

'He *does* claim to be acting in my interests . . .' Darren said in Dawes's defence.

'That's bollocks, and he knows it. He's suckering you. My job's to save your career, not his.'

'You *did* help him land this . . .' Darren reminded Nick.

'As a one-off, yeah. But that's history. For the immediate future, I'd classify him as surplus to requirements. Okay?'

Darren drifted away. None of this seemed helpful. Then he became aware of Nick offering his wine glass in a toast. 'Thieves like us,' Nick said reassuringly. 'While I think on – I've got *GQ* magazine coming out to do a nice upmarket piece on you!'

'Great timing, Nick!'

'Now, now – big feature, lots of photos, and a sympathetic tone . . . you need things like this!'

'All right . . . Who's doing it?' said Darren surrendering. It hardly mattered in the circumstances.

'Alex Somebody-or-other . . . he's ringing soon as he gets here.'

'Well, he'd better make it quick, hadn't he?' Darren said pointedly, feeling that even as he lunched, events completely outside his control were conspiring against him.

Indeed, what Darren might have had in mind was happening that very afternoon, as Kenny Dawes turned up uninvited on board Vice-President Gamez's motoryacht, moored in the harbour. Gamez took the intrusion in his stride, assuming the appearance of the coach on his day off was a coincidence.

'What can I do for you, Ken?' he asked, pouring Dawes a glass of cava and introducing him to his guests.

'Matter of protocol, really. I don't know whether you've had any contacts, but I took a call from England last night. A transfer enquiry . . .'

Gamez rose immediately and indicated that Dawes should join him on the jetty. He was not about to discuss club matters in front of anybody, not even close friends.

'The enquiry was about Darren,' Dawes confirmed as they strolled between two rows of expensive yachts and cruisers.

'We have heard nothing. I had breakfast with President Vaqueras this morning. He would have mentioned such a development.'

'You sure?' Dawes asked beadily, in the light of recent events.

'Look, he is a man I trust. He wants nothing but the best,' Gamez said, clearly a sailor who was unwilling to rock any boat on which his status depended.

'You knew about the Barresco signing then?'

'Of course.'

'But you didn't regard it as necessary to inform me?'

Gamez shrugged. 'It may have seemed a little impolite . . .'

Dawes nodded vigorously. 'You're not kidding!'

'But we had had an open bid in for this Uruguayan which goes back to well before you joined. His arrival merely completed a process that started long ago.'

'Any more in the pipeline that I should know about?' Dawes asked with heavy sarcasm. 'Perhaps on the coaching side?'

Gamez smiled. Here was the real reason for the visit. 'That is not on the agenda, Kenny.'

'Barresco seems to have brought a lot of his own people with him. Personal trainer, bodyguards . . . adding his old club manager to the entourage wouldn't be a complete surprise.'

'He is a highly strung guy. He needs to feel comfortable with the people around him. They were a contractual obligation he forced upon us, though we did insist that *he* paid their wages, not us.'

'I'm obliged to select him until further notice though, aren't I?'

'One game, one goal. His success cannot harm you. But if he fails . . .'

Dawes tried to unravel the code in the message.

'Do you want Darren out?' he asked, trying to establish one possibility.

Gamez's face gave nothing away.

'No. That is not in our minds. He has made a good impression by and large.'

'But what if I put him back in the side?'

'Be careful. That's all I will say. There may well be room for both Darren and Barresco in time . . .'

'They're centre-forwards! A breed apart. They don't mix. Certainly not in this team. I mean, I think Darren would try because he's an unselfish kid. But I don't think he'd enjoy it.'

They reached the end of the jetty, and paused for a moment to take in the glorious sweep of the harbour.

'Look, Kenny, I will be open with you. For the moment, Darren has lost the President's favour. But Barresco is his new toy. I'm sure you can read the situation correctly. Besides, as we all know – things change.'

Dawes nodded. 'What if this enquiry about Darren turns out to be serious?'

'Then we will discuss it. Just because you are both English, it does not mean that we look on you as Siamese twins,' Gamez said falling into one of the million traps the language set for a foreigner. 'If he goes, it does not reflect on you. We signed him before you came, remember?'

'Please – don't remind me of how powerless I am!' Dawes joked. Underneath, though, he'd ruthlessly analysed Gamez's words. There was no doubt that Darren's career was in jeopardy, but that his own was less so. The dilemma for Dawes was whether or not to accept the status quo, or try to manipulate events further. Or,

233

more brutally, whether to abandon Darren to his fate, or to protect a young man he had come to respect.

One of the snags in this scenario, however, was that Dawes had been lying about the transfer enquiry over Darren. It had been a complete fiction, designed to elicit a response which he'd now been able to gauge. The trouble was, if it was believed, it might set a real transfer saga in motion. Not for the first time in his life, Darren could be on his way without having the slightest inkling about it.

Chapter Twelve

Darren took Nick 'out on the town' that night. He didn't feel much like it, of course, but it was better than sitting in with Nick at the house, listening to him moan about the Spanish telly, or giving graphic accounts of his latest sexual conquest. Besides, it was the first time in ages that he could socialise with Nick as a 'single white male', once again, and he could now show him parts of the city that in the past would have landed him in deep trouble with Claire.

The first call was to a dungeon of a bar in the Barrio Gotic, and the prime purpose of the visit here was to play a practical joke on Nick. It worked perfectly. There'd been two well-dressed, immaculately made-up women sitting alone at a table. Nick had eyed them up, to be rewarded with toothsome smiles. On Darren's advice he'd smoothed his way over to them with a bottle of champagne and struck up a conversation while Darren made a brief trip to the toilets.

When Darren returned, Nick was becoming aware that he'd been set up, as the 'women' began talking in the deepest of voices. He saw Darren smirking and winking and chased him out of the bar into the dark alley outside.

'What a stroke to play on a friend!' Nick shouted. 'I could have died of heart-failure, and it would have been your fault!'

Darren was folding up with laughter. He knew that

many of Barcelona's transvestites were extremely convincing, but he'd never expected Nick, the man of experience, to be so totally taken in.

'The worst part was I fancied them both!'

'They certainly fancied you!' Darren blurted in between peals of laughter.

As recompense, Darren took Nick up to one of the slickest of designer bars in the Zona Alta, which also boasted a disco as an added attraction. It was an expensive joint, but that made it less likely that Darren would be disturbed or baited by curious Barca fans. Most of the women had no trouble recognising him though, and Nick was quick to appreciate the looks and the smiles coming their way, even though Darren seemed impervious to them.

'Fancy a dance?' Nick ased, trying to draw Darren's attention to the expectant posse of young women nearby.

'I think you should try it with a woman first. You know, to get back into the swing . . .'

Nick grimaced at the joke. And retaliated.

'So – what are you going to do about your love-life now?'

'Give it a rest, I think.'

'Get off! You could pull any bird in this bar, couldn't you? They're queueing up over there!'

'I don't need the aggravation at the moment.'

'Bit bruised, are we?' Nick asked with a lisp.

Darren refused to rise to the bait. 'I guess so. Claire and I had been together a long time. It's not easy to wipe the slate clean.'

'What if this Rafael geezer dumps her? Would you take her back?'

'Dunno. I *do* miss her. But I don't trust my own judgement at the moment. Whatever I did would probably be a mistake.'

'Yeah, you've got to sort your head out first. Get back in the team. Do what you do best. Score goals.'

Darren allowed himself an ironic smile. Despite all the money and sophistication it still came down to sticking a football in a net. 'Sure. "Do what you do best." Funny how people keep telling me that.'

'Well, makes you happy, doesn't it?'

'Oh, yes, in a pure, intense way too. As good as sex. Certainly more memorable.'

'They've got Samaritans over here, have they?' Nick asked with leaden irony. Darren slapped both his hands against his face, trying to snap out of his self-imposed gloom.

'Sorry. I'm not the best company at the moment.' He reached into his pocket and gave Nick a key.

'Spare key to the house. I'm gonna split.'

'Right you are. Bring one back for you, shall I?'

Darren climbed off his bar-stool. 'Yeah, but look out for six o'clock shadows this time.' Darren signed a few autographs as he left, and spoke to some of the girls who'd been eyeing him. But it was merely a courtesy. He just wasn't interested in meaningful contact. All that mattered for now was getting back his place in the team.

To that end, he rose early the next morning – there was no sign of Nick in the house – and took himself off on a long run up into the hills. The city looked utterly beautiful in the dawn sunlight, fuelling Darren's resolve to stay there. He pushed himself harder and harder on the run back to the house. If he was going to be left out of the team, he knew that it wouldn't be on the grounds of his fitness.

As he jogged loosely back through the gates of the house, a city taxi was pulling away empty. He checked his watch – it was nearing nine. Nick must have had quite a night.

237

'Go on, tell me all about it, you randy old bastard . . .' Darren called as he walked down the hall. Turning into the kitchen he found a smartly-dressed blonde woman in her late twenties, filling the coffee machine with water. Must be pretty special if Nick brought her home, he thought.

'Oh . . . *buenos dias* . . . *perdon!*' Darren muttered politely.

'Sorry – don't speak the lingo,' the woman said in metropolitan English. 'Your friend's gone up for a shower. I'm Alex Harper. From *GQ* magazine.'

'Oh – right. Er, I'm Darren. Matthews.'

Alex offered her hand. 'I recognise the legs.'

Darren wiped his right palm on his T-shirt and shook her hand, trying to get used to the idea that 'Alex' was not a man as he'd expected. That would teach him to play transvestite pranks on Nick.

'Your agent asked me to make some coffee . . .' Alex said returning to the machine.

'No, let me. Shit. I sound like a naff advert. Sorry I'm a mess.'

Alex smiled tolerantly. 'You look a lot better than your agent does.'

'Yeah, he was set on a good time when I left him last night.'

'Hence the "randy bastard" remark?'

'You won't put that in the article, I hope?'

Alex screwed up her face, teasing him. 'It'd be quite a good intro. Colourful. You speaking Spanish and all.'

Darren tried to assess what the old sea captains called 'the cut of her jib'. The last thing he wanted at the moment was some smart-arse journalist taking the piss out of his life-style by coming up with all the familiar footballer clichés.

'Right. I'll just go and jump in the bath,' he said

defensively. 'Help yourself to anything. I think there are some croissants in that cupboard.'

'Thanks,' Alex said, switching on the coffee machine.

Darren legged up the stairs, convinced she was going to put him over in a big way. He banged on the bathroom door from behind which low moaning sounds could be heard. Nick's face appeared looking pale and unshaven.

'Rough night?' Darren asked with clenched teeth.

Nick tried to recall events as best he could. 'I pulled a bird who wanted to go on to a disco at six in the morning. Even I had to wave the white flag at that.'

Darren pointed downstairs.

'I thought Alex was supposed to be a bloke?' he said accusingly.

'My secretary took the message. How was I supposed to know?' Nick managed a smirk. 'Fill your boots, son, she's tidy!'

'She's supposed to be writing a piece on my wonderful sophisticated life-style. So far she's got a puking middle-aged John Travolta-type and a sweaty oik in shorts! It'll read more like bedsit life in Shepherd's Bush than the fast lane in Barcelona!'

'Well schmooze her! Offer her a dip in the pool!' Nick began to blench. The retribution of the night was at hand. 'Sorry, too many Brandy Alexanders . . .' He closed the bathroom door.

Darren decided to take Alex down to the training ground and show her Nou Camp Stadium. As his Mercedes parked he could see Dawes and Vila watching, and he could virtually see what they were saying from a hundred yards away . . .

'Boss, boss – look! Now Stanley has his own personal trainer!' Vila squealed with delight.

'Been working on him all night by the look of it,' Dawes said leerily. They watched as Darren took Alex to a bench overlooking the training pitch and sat her down before heading for the changing-rooms. Unfortunately, to do this he had to pass Dawes and Vila, who were looking at him, eagerly awaiting explanations.

'Morning, Darren . . .' Dawes said in a sarky tone.

'Come here immediately, Stanley!' Vila demanded.

'She's just gonna watch the training, okay. It is a public session today, isn't it?'

'Depends who she's got her eye on, Darren.'

'Sorry, but Nick fixed it up. She's from *GQ* magazine.'

Dawes darkened. 'A journalist! I thought we'd put you straight about talking to them?'

'Not when they look like this one, boss,' Vila panted.

'Look, she's doing some kind of feature. She doesn't speak Spanish. And her piece won't be appearing for two months at least. By which time I may well be playing for Grimsby Town. Okay?'

Dawes recalled his conversation with Gamez, and wagged a finger at Darren. 'Be careful, Darren. Everything gets back to this club sooner or later, whatever language it's printed in. We're both on thin ice at the moment, but yours is over the deep end.'

Darren stood up close to Dawes, tiring of his lectures and warnings. 'Look, I don't need any advice from you, boss. All I want is my place back in the team . Can you deliver that yet?'

Dawes remained stony-faced. 'I've had a few words in the right sort of areas,' he said cryptically. 'I'm now waiting to get the nod from upstairs. But one false move and . . .' Dawes's gaze switched across to Alex.

'*Boss!* Time is running short. Nick is already making himself busy! I need a result!'

'Where is he?'

'Over at mine . . . talk to him, will you?'

240

Dawes opened his eyes wide. 'You're giving me orders?'

'I thought we had some sort of pact. All I'm getting from you is complacency because you seem to be off the hook!'

'I'm anything but, Darren! Now you leave this to me and concentrate on your training, will you?'

Darren jogged off towards the changing-rooms, noticing that Alex had been watching the conversation all too keenly.

The training session passed uneventfully, but gave Darren little encouragement. Barresco played for half an hour in the centre-forward position, so Darren was obliged to drop deeper. Neither he nor Barresco sparkled, so any Vaqueras spies in the watching group of fans would have gone away with little to report. After he'd showered Darren met up again with Alex, who'd been touring the F.C. Barcelona museum inside the stadium.

'Sorry to keep you.'

'No problem. I've been taking in the surroundings. Very impressive.'

They moved off towards the players' car-park.

'Don't suppose you got much out of the training session?' Darren asked, fishing.

'Well I don't know. At a rough guess, I'd say you and Mr Dawes weren't getting on. Right?'

'Lip-reader, eh?'

'More a student of body language. Most of the editors I've worked for use the same techniques – aggressive posture, a lot of pointing, making people come to them in order to display who has the power.'

Darren laughed, recognising many of these behavioural facets. 'But are we talking about me or Kenny Dawes?' he joked.

'Well, you seemed to be giving as good as you got.'

241

Darren paused for a moment. He was beginning to think he could trust Alex. She was no fool, for one thing, and also seemed refreshingly free of that traditional journalistic stance best summarised as 'talking down to, and looking down upon' the people whose time they were seeking. So he risked confiding in her.

'You realise this row will be resolved one way or another before your article comes out?'

'I'd bet on *you* winning.'

'You'd lose your money, I think,' Darren said in his usual self-deprecatory way.'

'Don't knock yourself. My brother was very excited when he heard I was flying out to meet you . . .'

'Does he fancy me or something?'

'He's a barrister. Football's made a social breakthrough in England, hasn't it? You've got bishops, judges, and Cabinet Ministers going to watch now.'

'Along with the power-crazed tycoons who've hijacked the game,' Darren insisted. He paused, and gestured back to the towering bowl of the Nou Camp.

'You see that – it was built with the subscriptions of the supporters. So every Barca fan owns it. The *club* belongs to them too. We're still light years behind that kind of development.'

Alex was watching Darren, not the stadium, sensing his enthusiasm. 'You really like it here, don't you?'

Darren shrank back a little, realising he'd probably given too much of himself away. But then that didn't bother him so much as the prospect of leaving the club. 'If only it was that easy . . .' he said, remembering how much work there was still to do.

Darren took Alex back to the house. They sat outside by the pool as she taped a more formal interview with him. It was an odd experience – she had a way of looking him directly in the eyes and coaxing truths from him. It wasn't down to a technique or anything. Alex just seemed to have a natural trustworthiness about her. She was trying to get a picture of his life beyond the idyll of football, sunshine and swimming pools.

'What if it rains? What do you do for entertainment out here?'

Darren shrugged. 'Don't give it much thought really. The city itself is enough. Just looking around, you know? Barcelona is it's own museum really. You can see five or six different centuries of history within a few square miles.'

'What about books?' Alex pressed.

Darren stroked his chin. 'Yes, they're those rectangular things made out of paper with stories in them.'

Alex smiled and shook her head. 'Stop it, Darren, you're not a thicko!'

'A "thicko"?' He hadn't heard that since schooldays. 'No, maybe not – but I'm not that educated either. You're university, I take it?'

Alex nodded. 'I *did* have to work in a chicken-factory during vacations to pay off my overdraft.'

'And I had you down as posh . . .'

'From Huddersfield? Not quite.'

'Must have worked hard then . . . to get there . . . ?'

Alex chastised him again. 'Darren, I'm supposed to be interviewing *you*!'

'Sorry. I don't feel like talking about myself at the moment. Where were we?'

'Well, the Englishman abroad has become such a figure of fun . . . I was just trying to find out how you'd avoided it?'

'Who said I had?'

'Come on – you can get by in the language, you've settled in the city . . . you're streets ahead of most Brits here. Twenty years in the country and they still won't use a word of Spanish. The *Daily Telegraph* and the postal vote are their idea of local culture.'

This seemed genuine praise, but it didn't help in the circumstances. 'Thanks, but Kenny Dawes is still in his job and I soon won't be, so maybe that stuff doesn't matter after all.'

'You know it does. Those fans outside the training ground this morning – they're desperate for you to stay. You're a hero.'

Darren nodded, quietly touched by these reports. 'Thanks . . .' He stretched and stood up. 'Do you want to go out for lunch, maybe? There's a nice place just down the road.'

Alex switched her tape off. 'I'm happy with a sandwich . . . or whatever.'

'I may be able to do that . . .' He headed back across the terrace towards the kitchen.

'Darren, would you mind if I had a swim?'

He turned. 'Er, no. Sure. I doubt if there's a cozzie though – the previous occupant . . .' His voice tailed off.

'I'll manage . . .'

Darren hesitated. 'I'll get you a towel.'

So while Darren busied himself making baguettes filled with a salad Niçoise, Alex skinny-dipped in the pool. Darren tried to keep his mind on the hard-boiled eggs and the tuna on the work surface. But he couldn't help but be aware, as he heard the water slapping gently in the pool, that for the first time since that dreadful night of separation with Claire, he was thinking about sex again.

He completed the two baguettes, placed them onto plates and found a tray. He selected two pairs of knives and forks, and took a bottle of white wine out of the fridge. He carried the tray to the doors then paused and called out, 'I'll be bringing the lunch out in a sec . . .'

He silently counted to ten, allowing her plenty of time to get out of the pool and into her towel. Then she suddenly appeared at the door, standing naked with her hair and body glistening with water.

'I, er, hope you like anchovies . . .' Darren said limply. Alex approached him as he stood awkwardly with the tray. She leant across and kissed him tenderly on the lips.

'Shall we take those to bed?'

Darren succumbed not just out of lust – that was slaked, a little embarrassingly, within a minute of them hitting the sheets – but because he'd stumbled upon someone he could trust a little. His world lately had been reduced to suppressing his emotions for fear of what capital people might make out of them – his parents, Nick, Dawes, journalists, all had vested interests in him one way or another. Now here was Alex, not trying to push him, or to be judgemental about him. It was a pleasant change.

He watched as she lay dreamily on his chest, her wet hair trailing right across it.

'You didn't set out to achieve this, did you?'

'No. Did you?'

'You're kidding. Couldn't score from two yards at the moment.'

'It's a pleasant surprise for both of us then. I came wanting to like you – and I did. I do.'

'Some footballers will do anything for good publicity, you know?'

Alex opened one eye. 'Who said you were good?' She stretched and rolled onto her side. 'Why do you think you've settled so well here?'

'We've resumed the interview now, have we?'

Alex nodded, mock business-like. Darren thought about her question. 'I dunno – I feel a kind of sympathy with the people, I suppose. Being provincial, I grew up always resenting being classed as second-rate because I didn't happen to come from London. I think there's

245

some of that defiance in the Catalan people. They want the world to know there's been more to Spain than Madrid!'

'Now you can tell them there's life after Huddersfield too.'

They both laughed intimately. Then the bloody bedside phone rang. They both reacted to the intrusion with disappointment.

'That'll be Nick, reporting on his pow-wow with Dawes.' Darren answered the phone. It wasn't Nick, but Jordi Bassas reporting on his complete failure to trace any relative of Darren's with a Catalan connection.

'Well – not to worry. It was always a long-shot. Thanks for trying, *amigo . . . adios . . .*'

Darren replaced the receiver.

'Bad news?' Alex enquired solicitously.

'Worse. *No* news,' said Darren.

But the bad news wasn't long in coming. Nick turned up later in the afternoon having had a chat with Dawes in which they'd discovered that they'd both set up fictional transfer enquiries to Barcelona for Darren, the combined effect of which would almost certainly be for it to look as though Darren himself was orchestrating his way out. Nick was seething, and had told Dawes to stay right out of Darren's life in future.

Darren paced the room, absorbing this latest downturn in his fortunes. Alex had stayed on, much to Nick's discomfort. The idea of talking business in front of a stranger, albeit one who'd just shagged his client, appalled him.

'It's all right, Nick. No secrets. Besides, there's not much point in Alex writing her feature if I'm about to give up here.'

Nick looked dubious. 'Well, if you want to know, my instinct would be to get out now. Knock it on the head.'

246

'I don't want your instinct, Nick – I want your advice.'

'My advice is, pack it up. You can't rely on any favours from Dawes. In fact, he's probably written you off already, just as I have written him off.'

'But it seems to me that Darren's very popular with the fans,' contributed Alex.

Young smiled patronisingly at her. 'Well, if they could see him play, darling, he might well be! But there's little chance of that under the present regime.'

'Terrific,' said Darren in a monotone.

'Listen, you can get back to England relatively undamaged. Most British players fail abroad, so there's no stigma. Best of all, I can use your present wage level as a way of negotiating top rates back in England.'

'What if I decide to stay put?'

'You tell me? The worst case scenario would be Kenny getting the boot, and Barresco's manager being brought in from Uruguay. You'd probably never get another game, *but* you'd be the highest paid non-playing footballer in Europe! If you can live with that, fine.'

Darren caught Alex's eye. 'You know I couldn't.'

'Then let me get weaving!' Nick begged. Darren scratched his head in dismay, and exhaled deeply.

Alex left for the airport shortly afterwards. They talked about meeting up again. The 'where' was a problem rather than the 'when'.

'You'll be all right, Darren. Just don't be bullied. Know what *you* want – and do anything to achieve it,' she said softly to him before kissing him lingeringly. He held on to her for several minutes, afraid of letting her go. But then she broke away and in seconds the taxi was gone.

The training session the next morning virtually sealed Darren's fate – at least that's what he thought. He'd imposed himself on Barresco during the match, trying to play alongside him, especially as Vaqueras was watching from the touchline. But the little Uruguayan was touchy about his space – he niggled at Darren and gestured his frustration so graphically that soon Dawes was being summoned to the touchline again by the President.

The orders were basically for Darren to stay out of Barresco's way. Darren trooped off to the wing and the play resumed. When a neat passing move saw Barresco break free on goal, with Darren unmarked to his right, the Uruguayan preferred to shoot at the goalkeeper rather than risk giving Darren a goal. Darren left the session, feeling isolated and abandoned. Maybe Nick was right – it was time to go home.

Later in the week he met up with Claire at her invitation. Her choice of venue – the cable-car station in the harbour – suggested that she had nothing more intimate on her mind than a tourist trip. Just one more thing to tick off the list – might as well do it with Darren. That's how bleak he felt.

As the car jerked out of the station and hung out over the sea, it began to rise up towards the hill of Montjuic. The panorama of the city was astonishing. Darren watched blankly.

'Things are getting worse, are they?' guessed Claire.

'Could well be on my way home. Nick wants it anyway.'

'Darren, I'm sorry. You don't, presumably?'

He gestured to the city. 'Look at this place, Claire. Anywhere else is downhill!' He turned to her, gave her a resigned smile.

'At least *you've* got a result. What's happening with the designs?'

Claire fished in her handbag and handed him an invite – it wasn't just tourism. The text was simple:

'Rafael Jiminez invites you to a Private View of new work by Claire Travis'. Darren took this in. 'You've got a show?' Claire nodded modestly. 'What with models and that?'

'Well, one or two. It's only a small party. I hope you can come.'

'I'd have to meet Rafael, I suppose.'

'I think you'll like him, despite all. I'll understand if you can't make it.'

'So will I,' he said pointedly, before apologising. 'Sorry. So all the tears and the snot were worthwhile then?'

'For me, yes. I just hope things work out for you.'

'Well I'm trying. God knows, I'm trying.' He turned away to take in the view again. 'I, er, I did meet somebody nice the other day . . .'

'Tell me!' said Claire eagerly.

'Too early yet. May just have been a holiday romance. All depends on what happens at the club. With my luck, I'll get a move to Sporting Tehran – no women, no booze, just the odd camel for company.'

Claire admonished him for a whole range of '-isms', and for being miserable.

'I'm all right. Really. Look. A smile. I'll miss having you as a mate if I have to go back.'

'So will I,' Claire said tenderly.

Darren looked at her appreciatively. They were a hundred feet up over the sea now. And alone. 'There was a time when I'd now be inviting you to join the kilometre high club . . .'

Claire gave him no encouragement. 'Before you try and complicate things, Rafael asked me to get two tickets for the Madrid game off you.'

Darren gave her a beady look. 'I'll see what I can do. Maybe if I put him in the Madrid end . . .'

As the countdown to the big game began, Nick began

calling round the big English Premier League clubs, not to mention Rangers in Glasgow, alerting them to Darren's situation. Darren was cooking him a Spanish version of a fry-up breakfast, listening to his hustling, when the front doorbell rang insistently.

Darren headed off down the hall and opened the door. Jordi Bassas stood there, out of breath, agitated, his car parked with its engine still running.

'Darren – get in! Quick,' he demanded.

Darren shouted back up the hall to Nick, 'Can you get your own breakfast!' and ran off.

In the newspaper offices, Bassas revealed what he had found – a late 1970s edition of his paper, featuring a leading Catalan politician presenting an award in London to an Englishman, Alfred Matthews.

'I was looking only through the Civil War years! And then I realised – it could only have taken place after Franco's death in '75.'

Bassas showed Darren photos on a screen. A ghostly image suddenly appeared of Alfred Matthews. Bassas translated the headline: 'Catalonia Salutes an English Hero – Alfred Matthews!'

Bassas ran the story the next day, complete with photos of both Darren and his uncle. Within hours, Darren was summoned to Vaqueras's home at his vineyard near Vilafranca.

Darren put on his club blazer and drove inland out to the hills, every one of which was dotted with vines. He found 'Bodegas Vaqueras' and headed up a long drive to an eighteenth-century house. An atmosphere of timeless calm hung over the place.

Darren was escorted out onto a terrace where Vaqueras was sitting at a table, one of his bottles in front of him. That Vaqueras's attitude to Darren had changed was indicated by the fact that he ignored his handshake and hugged Darren like a son.

'Darren! Why didn't you tell me about your uncle? I was very touched to read his story!'

'So was I, Senor President. I really didn't know much about it.'

Vaqueras poured the wine. 'Your uncle was a great man, Darren! Helping many Catalonians through a regrettable time in our history.'

'It's a shame I was too young to remember him before he died.'

'Well, yes . . . but you too are now serving the Catalonion nation in your own way! Indeed, this country is already yours, my boy – you appreciate our history, our language, our food . . . and our wine! Above all, you know what identity and passion we find in our football. To you, Darren . . . one more Catalonian!'

Darren felt dizzy with praise. Now he found out what this all translated into.

'Now, because of these great omens, Darren, you will return to the team against Real Madrid . . . as centre-forward!'

'With respect, Senor President – I hope I'm being selected on merit . . .' Darren stammered but inside, his heart was pumping already at the thought of the game.

He wasn't to be disappointed. The stadium was full two hours before the kick-off – 120,000 supporters waving the flags of Barca and Catalonia and screaming their defiance of Madrid. As the teams came out, the noise was deafening – klaxons sounding, crowd roaring, thunder-flashes going off.

Darren barely remembered the match apart from his goal that won the game for Barca – a diving header from a cross in by Barresco. After that it was like being a cork in a whirlwind. The noise nearly knocked him over, his senses utterly swamped.

After the match hundreds of thousands thronged the

streets, jamming up the city. People hung out of every window of every flat, out of every window of every car, waving giant Catalan flags, sounding klaxons, banging drums.

By now Darren had retired to a hotel terrace with Nick and others. They watched the mad carnival below.

'Look, I hate to break up the party mood, but I had a call this afternoon. From Blackburn Rovers. Five-year contract. Name your wage. House and car thrown in. You interested, Darren?'

Darren gave nothing away. 'What? And give up showbusiness?' he said with a grin.